COLL
VALUE

HARMONY®
KINGDOM

**Collector Handbook and
Secondary Market Price Guide**

FIRST EDITION

This publication is *not* affiliated with The Harmony Ball Company® or any of their affiliates, subsidiaries, distributors or representatives. Any opinions expressed are solely those of the authors, and do not necessarily reflect those of The Harmony Ball Company. Harmony Kingdom®, *Treasure Jests*® and *Lord Byron's Harmony Garden*® are registered trademarks of The Harmony Ball Company. *Angelique*™, *Harmony Circus*™, *The Garden Party*™ and *Picturesque*™ are also trademarked by The Harmony Ball Company. All Harmony Kingdom artwork is the copyrighted property of The Harmony Ball Company.

Managing Editor:	Jeff Mahony	Creative Director:	Joe T. Nguyen
Associate Editors:	Melissa A. Bennett	Production Supervisor:	Scott Sierakowski
	Jan Cronan	Senior Graphic Designers:	Lance Doyle
	Gia C. Manalio		Susannah C. Judd
	Paula Stuckart		David S. Maloney
Contributing Editor:	Mike Micciulla		Carole Mattia-Slater
Editorial Assistants:	Jennifer Filipek	Graphic Designers:	Jennifer J. Bennett
	Nicole LeGard Lenderking		Sean-Ryan Dudley
	Joan C. Wheal		Peter Dunbar
Research Assistants:	Timothy R. Affleck		Kimberly Eastman
	Priscilla Berthiaume		Jason C. Jasch
	Heather N. Carreiro		David Ten Eyck
	Beth Hackett	Web Graphic Designer:	Ryan Falis
	Victoria Puorro		
	Steven Shinkaruk		
Web Reporters:	Samantha Bouffard		
	Ren Messina		

ISBN 1-888-914-83-1

306 Industrial Park Road • Middletown, CT 06457
www.collectorbee.com

Contents

Contents

Introducing The Collector's Value Guide™

Since their unveiling in 1995 at the International Collectible Exposition in Long Beach, California, Harmony Kingdom's tiny intricate boxes have become one of the hottest collectibles in the industry. Along with a new millennium, the year 2000 promises to bring many exciting announcements and surprises for Harmony Kingdom collectors, including the first edition of The Collector's Value Guide™ to Harmony Kingdom® which promises to provide current information to keep dedicated fans up to date.

In this guide, you will be taken on a tour through the enchanting and often quirky world of Harmony Kingdom, past and present, and be provided with up-to-date information on secondary market values, new releases and retirements. This Collector's Value Guide™ is filled with everything you need to help make your Harmony Kingdom collection a dream come true, and is bound to become a treasured companion in your collecting adventure.

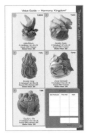

Look inside to find:

- **The first glimpse of two new Harmony Kingdom series:** *Mini Treasure Jests* **and** *NetsUKes*

- **Up close and personal interviews with two of the people who started it all: Noel Wiggins and Martin Perry**

- **Every piece pictured in full-color with essential information, including its value and artist**

- **The latest news concerning the Royal Watch Collector's Club**

- **The new pieces for 2000**

    And much, much more!

Through The Wilds Of Harmony Kingdom®

Harmony Kingdom has grown into one of the hottest lines of collectibles on the market. But it wasn't always this way. These amazing carvings are the creations of many visionary individuals, all of whom started down different paths until a combined passion for creativity united them, and they introduced Harmony Kingdom to the world at large.

In the early 1980s, Noel Wiggins and Lisa Yashon met at Brown University in Rhode Island and formed a friendship. Six years later, that friendship sent them on an adventure that would eventually make them business partners. The two set out for Mexico, where they became fascinated with the miniatures and folk art found in the markets and shops. Upon returning to the United States, Wiggins and Yashon sold the many trinkets they had gathered in Mexico. A year later, the two decided to concentrate on jewelry, and soon after that, The Harmony Ball Company was created. By 1991, the new company was employing hundreds of Mexican artists and selling an enormous amount of sterling silver earrings, pendants and necklaces. Everyone loved them and as a result, many people tried to copy the designs. The two friends realized that they needed a line of items that would be produced in a limited quantity and be subject to the copyright laws.

In the meantime, across the Atlantic in England, Martin Perry was working in his one room studio making replicas of other works. As his ability and passion for creating started to flourish, Perry soon began to create his own pieces from netsukes to animal box figurines. He soon formed his own production company, Antiquark Ltd., in 1989, dealing mostly on a local level. In 1990, Peter Calvesbert was hired as Antiquark's master carver. He and Perry sculpted pieces that were sold to Studio Ann Carlton which would then add their own finishing touches and sell them as their own.

In early 1994, Wiggins and Yashon were in Europe looking for ways to branch out their jewelry business. It was at a gift show in Germany, where they found a booth selling the animal boxes, that Wiggins and Yashon knew they had finally found what they were looking for. They immediately tracked down the source, Martin Perry, and inquired about forming a new company to distribute the quirky boxes worldwide. Not long after, the three began their evolution into a company which would bring the world a whole new kind of collectible.

The first Harmony Kingdom pieces to make it to the United States weren't like the boxes we know today. These early pieces were jewelry boxes, literally – each one contained a small pendant or gem of some kind, tying Perry and Calvesbert's carvings to Wiggins and Yashon's jewelry. It wasn't long before Harmony Kingdom retailers realized that these boxes were beautiful and whimsical by themselves, with no jewelry inside. Stores began to ask only for the boxes, and the line called *Treasure Jests* was born.

While enjoying moderate success, those in charge of Harmony Kingdom were still new to the world of collectibles. It wasn't until a year later that they gave organization to the set of 60 pieces. The were given memorable names, organized into different lines and some were even retired. When the collection was displayed in April 1995 at the Long Beach International Collectible Exposition, it was official – Harmony Kingdom had taken the collectibles world by storm.

> **LORD BYRON GOES TO CHINA**
>
> Production of *Lord Byron's Harmony Garden* was moved from Griffin Mill in England to China in 1997. The boxes had become very intricate and complex and moving the production location gave artists more freedom to continue creating the adventures of the little ladybug.

But if one wants to put out a lasting line of collectible items, diversity is required. Harmony Kingdom decided to branch out and create new items, and to do that, a new sculptor was needed. Former commercial artist David Lawrence was the perfect choice, and in 1995, he crafted his first holiday pieces. Lawrence would also go on to create the *Angelique* line and the crazy characters of *Harmony Circus*. Lawrence is also the creator of the *Zookeepers* collection. Harmony Kingdom was quickly becoming more than just a line of boxes and figurines – it was becoming art.

Another exciting series of boxes joined Harmony Kingdom in 1997. *Lord Byron's Harmony Garden* gives collectors an exciting field of flowers to choose from, as well as an opportunity to follow the interesting tales of a ladybug as the interior scenes depict ladybug Lord Byron's adventures. Each release is considered a "Chapter," and Lord Byron's future experiences remain a mystery until the next Chapter blossoms – with maybe a clue or two carved into the pieces of the previous chapter which hint at what those adventures may be.

In the Summer of 1999, collectors were introduced to a new and unique part of Harmony Kingdom – a collection of tiles called *Picturesque*. So far, there are three series: *Noah's Park*, the inaugural series, followed by *Byron's Secret Garden*, both of which were released in July. The third series is called *Wimberley Tales* and is new for 2000. All three series contain 20 tiles, which can be purchased separately or as a group.

Collecting is not merely a hobby. For many people, it is a way of life! Since 1995, Harmony Kingdom has given collectors a way to really join the Harmony Kingdom community with its Royal Watch Collector's Club. Members of the club receive exclusive benefits ranging from special event pieces, to membership pieces, to a quarterly newsletter called *The Queen's Courier*.

The club is constantly offering new and exciting ways for Harmony Kingdom devotees on both sides of the Atlantic to feel like part of the family. There are also Independent Clubs. Initiated by collectors themselves, these clubs offer Harmony Kingdom enthusiasts a way to come together on a local, regular basis, sharing personal stories and collections. So far, there are 25 Independent Clubs throughout the United States and United Kingdom, which are official-ly sanctioned by The Harmony Ball Company. Each holds meetings, sends out newsletters to members, and sponsors charitable events to raise money for the charity of its choice. In May 1999, the House of Peers was created as a liaison between Harmony Kingdom and the clubs. One person from each Independent Club is elected to become a member of the House of Peers, which oversees the progress of the clubs.

Welcome to the

HK

HOUSE of PEERS

House of Peers

(The House of Lords is the second chamber of the British Houses of Parliament. Members of the House of Lords are known as 'peers'.)

In this day and age, almost every-one and everything is accessible via the Internet, and Harmony Kingdom is no different. In late 1996, Harmony Ball Company was the first collectibles company to set up an Internet chat room offering fans all over the globe a place to share and compare stories about their favorite pieces! Now, the official Harmony Kingdom web site, *www.harmonyking-dom.com* offers everything from new releases to retailer locations to information on artist signings. Members of the Royal Watch Collector's Club and the Independent Clubs can also find information on-line.

Wanting to give collectors even more, Harmony Ball Company goes farther than most other companies. In 1997, collectors attending the International Collectible Exposition at Rosemont had the opportunity to board the Eleanor R cruise ship for

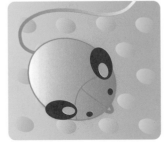

"The Three Hour Tour." In 1998, they embarked upon "The Ugly Duckling" cruise. And in 1999, they traveled back to Medieval Times to attend "Harmony Kingdom's Grand Investiture."

In April 1999, it sponsored the first annual convention at sea! Calling the excursion the "Primordial Crooze," the artists and representatives of Harmony Kingdom and Harmony Ball Company joined their legions of fans on a five day luxury cruise from Long

Beach, California to Mexico. Collectors not only got the chance to get up-close-and-personal with the artists, but also attended seminars, watched an actual carving of a piece (later to be available only to crooze goers), and even

learned how to make a box of their own. This year, the convention promises to be bigger and better. Located on the beautiful Lake Geneva in Wisconsin, the Clair de Lune 2000 Convention will be full of surprises, including workshops, artist signings and swap & sells. Collectors attending the four day event will receive "Clair de Lune," an exclusive box figurine. Not only is this piece special because it's exclusive to those who attend the convention, but it also is the inaugural piece to the *Clair de Lune* series premiering in the new millennium.

Besides the new *Clair de Lune* series, Harmony Kingdom has lots of things in store for its collectors for the new millennium. The year kicks off with a new series of *Treasure Jests*. The new *Mini* box figurines are now the smallest of the group, but they promise to hold just as much quirkiness and humor as the rest of the boxes. Another special addition is a series of *NetsUKes*. The first six of these solid-bodied animal figurines (not boxes!) will make their debut in the new millennium as well.

As Harmony Kingdom grew in the field, so did their need for more physical space to grow within. During the early part of 1998, Harmony Kingdom began saying goodbye to its home in Griffin Mill, and prepared for its move to its brand new home in Wimberley Mills. The extra space and new scenery will certainly allow for future growth and artistic inspiration. And this is welcomed news for collectors.

From its humble beginnings as, quite literally, a cottage industry in the rolling rural hills of England, Harmony Kingdom has since grown to encompass a collectibles empire and a devout following of collectors. Noel Wiggins, Lisa Yashon and Martin Perry surely never dreamed it would get this big, nor could Peter Calvesbert and David Lawrence have foreseen that their imaginations would have taken the line this far. But that's exactly what has happened within the strange, whimsical and beautiful world of Harmony Kingdom – a place where crabs lure their lunch with sandwiches, where the flowers bloom all year and the crazy circus never ends.

A Charitable Kingdom

For more than five years, Harmony Kingdom has gained an incredible amount of support from its fans. Now, Harmony Kingdom is giving back to a society which has helped make the line the so successful. Through the creation of the House of Peers in May 1999, Harmony Kingdom has been able to raise almost

$19,000 through various auctions and raffles for several charitable organizations. Although this is not the sole mission of the House of Peers, it represents The Harmony Ball Company's commitment to charity on the national level.

The House of Peers officially debuted in May 1999. Earlier that month, a series of devastating and deadly tornados ripped through the Midwest. On May 26, the House of Peers offered a prototype of "Roadkill," part of the *Black Box* series, for auction on eBay. When the auction ended, the piece had sold for $4,085 – all of which went to Feed The Children, a relief organization dedicated to feeding the hungry. The money was given as part of a major relief effort to aid Oklahoma City tornado victims.

In June 1999, the House of Peers held its second charitable event, this time in the presence of the Independent Clubs during the Rosemont International Collectible Exposition at "Harmony Kingdom's Grand Investiture." The piece raffled was a unique version of "Close Shave." A total of $5,640 was raised, and went to the winner's Independent Club's charities: American Diabetes Association, Make-A-Wish Foundation and World Wildlife Fund.

Queen Empress dealers hosted in-store events to auction or raffle off two

"Chucky Pig" pieces donated by The Harmony Ball Company in August of 1999. The events raised a total of $82,000 and the proceeds went to charities ranging from The American Cancer Society to local missions and shelters.

The third raffle, held in September 1999, gave more collectors a chance to win rare prototypes of their favorite pieces – the raffle consisted of four drawings. Like the "Close Shave" raffle, this event raised money for the winning independent charities. The four pieces, donated by Martin Perry and The Harmony Ball Company, were "Aria Amorosa," "Murphy's Last Stand," "Straight From The Hip" and "The Mouse That Roared." The event raised a total of $3,605, and the proceeds went to each of the winner's club's chosen charities.

In October 1999, Harmony Kingdom again came to help the efforts of people struck by tragedy. In accordance with The American Red Cross, a prototype angel was offered for auction on eBay to raise funds for victims of Hurricane Floyd. "A 'Naked' Angel" is one of only eleven in existence, part of a series of "risqué" angels that never made it into production. This particular piece was painted by Martin Perry, perhaps another reason it was so successful in raising more than $5,600 dollars, all of which was distributed to flood victims by The American Red Cross.

Harmony Kingdom not only feels strongly about giving back to its collectors, but to nature as well. It demonstrates this through its *Zookeepers* and *Wee Beasties* program. In conjunction with the Brookfield Zoo in Illinois and the Pelican Island Preservation Society in Florida, Harmony Kingdom allows those who purchase a *Zookeepers* piece to adopt animals at either of these places. As a result, they will receive an exclusive *Wee Beasties* figurine, a small replica of the *Zookeepers* piece. The program was created ". . . to promote awareness and support for animal conservation organizations."

Meet The Artists

Martin Perry did not grow up with a dream of becoming an artist. When he was a young teenager, he left school and worked with his uncle in the film industry. Not satisfied with that way of life, he moved to the beautiful mountains of Wales and spent the next several years working in one of the least lucrative occupations in the world – sheepherding. Living in the isolated Welsh hills, he worked mostly for free. Although Perry continued his bucolic endeavors after meeting his wife, he eventually gave it up. He went to work for an art replication firm where he discovered a newfound joy in creating. It wasn't long before Perry went out on his own and began Antiquark Ltd., a tiny home-based company. He produced mostly items created from netsuke and oriental ivory molds, which he gave to friends. As his pieces began to grow in popularity, the carvings became more and more complex. It wasn't long before he hired Peter Calvesbert, and the two began crafting their popular *Treasure Jests*. In fact, the line proved to be so popular that eventually outside companies asked to manufacture the boxes while Perry and his new master carver created the designs. A contract was signed with Studio Ann Carlton, which Perry cancelled in 1995. Not much later that the two artists joined forces with Noel Wiggins and Lisa Yashon to bring us Harmony Kingdom as we now know it.

Peter Calvesbert came to Antiquark when founder Martin Perry found his company growing in leaps and bounds. Like Perry, he did not aspire to be an artist early in life. In fact, he went to work for Martin Perry on a whim. But a slight background in ceramics prepared him for his present calling, and his incredible imagination did the rest. Calvesbert expresses his profound fascina-

tion with the animal kingdom in nearly all of his creations. His inspiration comes from such creatures as whales he has seen frolicking off Cape Cod, toads who take up residence outside his home, and even his now famous dog, Murphy. His trademark signature is a feisty mouse that often turns up on most of the *Treasure Jest* boxes. Calvesbert expresses his personal life into his creations as well. At the time of his marriage to his wife Andrea, members of the Royal Watch Collector's Club were treated to the special carving "The Big Day," a bride-and-groom likeness of the couple. Since then, he has followed up with the appropriate anniversaries: "Paper," "Cotton," "Leather" and "Silk Anniversary," each humorously depicting his ongoing married life.

D avid Lawrence's background as a medical illustrator prepared him for London's world of advertising. Despite the profitability of the field, he longed to spend his energies on something more personally fulfilling. Lawrence left London for the English countryside and moved into a home dating back to the late 1600s and pursued his need for creativity. Harmony Kingdom fit the bill. David Lawrence's creations add another dimension to the Harmony Kingdom line. His first creation, "Chatelaine," was

Harmony Kingdom's first *Holiday* figurine. He is also known for his *Angelique* collection, in which he immortalizes his daughter Rose and her neighborhood friends, and the *Zookeepers* collection. However, *Harmony Circus* is the line for which David Lawrence is best known. With some imagination and humor, and a lot of freedom from Martin Perry, he created a fabulous cast of crazy characters and brilliant designs.

Monique Baldwin is one of the artists responsible for the creation of Lord Byron's Harmony Garden. Dominican-born, Baldwin moved to Stroud in Gloucestershire, England very early in life, and remained there while studying design. She furthered her training at Carmarthen College in Wales, and before long was working in Harmony Kingdom's Finishing Department and later moved from department to department so that she can learn all that she could about the production process. When her work was noticed by Martin Perry, he made her his assistant and in turn, helped create many of the intricate inner designs for the first three chapters of Harmony Garden's Lord Byron's Adventures. The detailed "Rose Bud" is Baldwin's first solo piece, and she can proudly boast that Chapter 4 was her own creation.

Mark Ricketts took some time for him to decide what he wanted to do with his life. When he decided to become an artist, he originally wanted "to create extravagant civic works that would be seen for miles and miles." But devotees of Harmony Kingdom should be grateful that he never got to "paint the cliffs of Dover white" as he desired. Instead, he got serious about learning the techniques of art and went to work on creating miniature-sized figurines. Ricketts' boundless creativity eventually found an outlet when he met Martin Perry, and helped carve Chapter One of *Lord Byron's Harmony Garden*. Perry was aware of Ricketts' ability to relay human expression in small proportions, and decided to give him a more delicate task. Together, the two created *Wimberley Tales*, the third series of tiles in the *Picturesque* collection.

Ann Richmond grew up near the present headquarters of Harmony Kingdom. She acquired two things early in life which influenced her forever – a fondness for nature and a talent for painting. Her artistic talent grew into a successful career before she became involved with Harmony Kingdom. She quickly gained popularity locally, and was soon involved in a partnership that promoted herself, as well as other sculptors. As for her ties to Harmony Kingdom, she is responsible for sculpting the first two series in the *Picturesque* tile collection: *Byron's Secret Garden* and *Noah's Park*.

Sherman Drackett is one of the most recent additions to the line-up of Harmony Kingdom's talented artists. His intense creativity, his stint in the British Army and extensive travel created the inspiration that helped him master the membership pieces for the 2000 Royal Watch Collector's Club: "Field Day," "Lover's Leap" and "Merry-Go-Round." Ricketts has always wanted to be an artist. He says when he was a teenager, he would sit in his art classes and dream of becoming a sculptor. He expanded that love and became involved with "sugar craft," a talent which won him an entry into the "Hotel Olympia Salon Collinair Exhibition," one of Europe's finest competitions.

Julie Bharucha also has recently provided her artistic abilities to Harmony Kingdom. She has the honor of creating the new "Clair de Lune" box figurine, the first in the *Clair de Lune* series which will debut in 2000. Bharucha is a potter who resides near Wimberley Mills. When Martin Perry met her, they two discussed the full-figured women whom the *Clair de Lune* pieces would depict. The *Clair de Lune* pieces intertwine Perry's ideas with Bharucha's own unique style, and promises to be an exciting new series.

Together, these creative talents are a major part of what makes Harmony Kingdom what it is. And they have become part of the line as well. At collectible shows, fans wait for hours to have the artists sign their pieces. And it is the artists' enthusiasm to do so, as well as to take the time to chat with these fans, that has made Harmony Kingdom a line about not only boxes, but of personalities and interaction.

While each artist brings very different experience, personality and creative insight to the line, each one is an equal part of an equation that equals Harmony Kingdom.

Behind The Scenes With Noel Wiggins

CheckerBee Publishing had the opportunity to speak with Harmony Kingdom co-owner Noel Wiggins about the line and its inception. Through his often tongue-in-cheek responses, Noel Wiggins gives collectors wonderful insight into just what makes Harmony Kingdom so popular.

CheckerBee: Can you tell us a little about your childhood?

N. Wiggins: My father was a diplomat so my childhood was very exotic. I lived in Panama (where I had a three toed sloth named Pepe), Sicily, France, Morocco, Malta, Switzerland and Washington D.C. My older brother was my compadre and we used to pal around and get into all kinds of mischief. I was always a quick learner and usually a disruptive element in the class room.

CheckerBee: I understand you studied film at Brown. How did you become interested in that art form?

N. Wiggins: I come from a fairly well known line of landscape painters (J. C. Wiggins, Guy C. Wiggins, Guy A. Wiggins) and was always interested in art growing up. After winning a prestigious art prize in France, my parents thought that the Wyeth family, famous for it's successive three generations of artists was going to be beat by four generations of Wiggins. But alas, I took an interest in film making and by extension, business so the painting has been put aside ... for now. I loved film because it seemed like such a great medium for telling stories. Harmony Kingdom is also about expression and story telling.

CheckerBee: Do you still consider yourself a student of film? Can you watch a movie without critiquing it?

N. Wiggins: After being immersed for four years in French film polemics, the pleasure I get from going to the movies is critiquing them. I have managed to spend my life without owning a TV set, so going out to see a film is an especially powerful experience for me.

CheckerBee: Rumor has it that you have always been somewhat of a collector yourself. What kind of stuff did you collect?

N. Wiggins: I first started collecting stamps as a child. I specialized in 19th century tobacco tax stamps and was a real fanatic. I then progressed to, of all things, late 50s, early 60s Barbie dolls, with a twin passion for TV personality action figures. I learned through these experiences that the act of hunting for something that is hard to find is one of the main thrills of collecting. Harmony Kingdom has quite a few designs that were never made in large quantities to keep this primal emotion alive: bragging rights.

CheckerBee: It was at Brown University that you met Lisa Yashon, co-owner of The Harmony Ball Company. What was your first meeting like?

N. Wiggins: I was listening to my boom box, blaring a rap song and she came over to say hi.

CheckerBee: I understand that the two of you worked on many projects together before founding The Harmony Ball Company. What can you tell us about those endeavors?

N. Wiggins: We worked on two films, peddled beer in Central Park, and sold handicrafts to pay for our adventures in Mexico.

CheckerBee: After Brown, you spent some time as a motorcycle messenger in New York City. Do you have any memorable experiences from that time that you'd like to share?

N. Wiggins: I used to wear a long woolen cape with yellow jodhpurs and knee high riding boots (an urbanite's concept of Pony Express gear) and I was once delivering a package to JFK Airport and the police thought I looked so strange that they got me mixed up with a potential terrorist and I was thrown, outfit and all, in the Brooklyn clink for the night!

CheckerBee: Do you remember the moment that you decided to head out to Ohio and take that monumental trip with Lisa that planted the seed for The Harmony Ball Company?

N. Wiggins: I had been to a store in New York called Little Rickies that sold little clay skeletons, "Calaveras," that the Mexicans make to commemorate their Day of the Dead festivities. I found out from the retailer as much as I could, called Lisa, and we were down in Mexico the following month.

CheckerBee: Was there any one thing that prompted you to make the transition from film to business?

N. Wiggins: Poverty!

CheckerBee: Your original business plans were not what we have come to know as The Harmony Ball Company. What can you tell us about these early ideas?

N. Wiggins: Originally Lisa and I were going to start a cafe/restaurant/film club with a Mexican flair called The Hereafter (still our corporate name), but we both aren't very good cooks so that idea was left on simmer. We still dream of doing a theme restaurant one day.

CheckerBee: Have you always had an interest in folk art?

N. Wiggins: I've always loved folk art. My current favorite is a Columbus, Ohio based artist named Rick Borg. Great stuff! I am profoundly jealous of the folk art collection that the restaurant House of Blues has.

CheckerBee: I understand that your original foray into marketing and selling jewelry faced some complications – some starts and stops. Were there times when you just wanted to give up the entire idea?

N. Wiggins: Not that I can remember. It's all too much fun.

CheckerBee: The Harmony Kingdom that we know today has much to do with your meeting Martin Perry. What can you tell us about that first encounter?

N. Wiggins: We met for the first time in New York at the Gift Show. We had been communicating before then by phone (and doing a fair bit of business). When we first saw each other we both laughed because he thought I was some big business man instead of a 27 year old kid at the Jacob Javitz Center!

CheckerBee: How did you and Lisa arrive at the name Harmony Kingdom?

N. Wiggins: It was a logical extension of Harmony Ball (which was a logical extension of a magazine we put out in college called *Harmony Magazine*).

CheckerBee: What qualities do you look for in a Harmony Kingdom artist?

N. Wiggins: Must have a terrific sense of humor and be very sensitive to the animal and human condition.

CheckerBee: How do you come up with the ideas and themes for the pieces?

N. Wiggins: A lot of clowning around and head banging!

CheckerBee: I've been told that there's a story behind every box. Where do these stories come from?

N. Wiggins: Much like a rock band we all have our different touches.

CheckerBee: I also understand that there are "secrets" hidden on or in the boxes as well. Is everyone privy to these secrets?

N. Wiggins: Only Royal Watch Club members can hear those!

CheckerBee: Many of the boxes have different, intentionally created versions. Why is this?

N. Wiggins: We see the first 5,000 pieces of a design (Version 1) as the edition where we can put commercial concerns on the back burner and really go all out and "push the envelope." Version 1s are made for our hardcore collectors. The next edition (Version Infinity) is made for the general gift market and tends to be considerably toned down – but very cute.

 CheckerBee: You take many chances with some of your designs – I have heard them called "controversial." Do you ever feel that you may be pushing things too far?

N. Wiggins: We get a big kick out of pushing things too far. Just wait for next year's *Black Box*.

CheckerBee: Do you have a favorite Harmony Kingdom piece?

N. Wiggins: My favorite box is the bull dogs called "Dead Ringer" because it is both elegant and extremely funny. To me it embodies what we are all about.

CheckerBee: Harmony Kingdom has a huge fan following as shown by the numerous collector clubs in existence and your booth's attendance at collector shows. When did you first realize that you had attained such success and were you surprised by it?

N. Wiggins: We are always happily surprised by the ribald enthusiasm of our fans. I feel as long as we all really love the product then there will always be like minded souls out there.

CheckerBee: You, Lisa and the artists have become celebrities in the collectibles industry. Did you ever expect this type of fame?

N. Wiggins: No, but it's the perfect amount of fame – people only recognize us at the Rosemont Convention Center!

CheckerBee: From the beginning, you have understood the power of the Internet. What can you say about the impact it has had on Harmony Kingdom?

N. Wiggins: The Internet has enabled us to reach out to people who share the same vision as we do. Because Harmony Kingdom is not intended for mass consumption, the line appeals to a smaller demographic than a standard collectible. Thus the Internet has enabled us to spread the word to our core following.

CheckerBee: Harmony Kingdom's success shows no signs of slowing down. Can you give us a hint at what the future holds for the company?

N. Wiggins: Children's books, animated movies, theme parks and lots more boxes!

CheckerBee: You are involved in so many aspects of the company, but there must be one part that you find particularly satisfying. What would that part be?

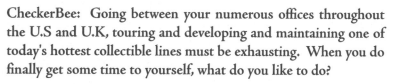

N. Wiggins: Talking to collectors and hearing their likes and dislikes. I also love buying the latest laptops!

CheckerBee: Going between your numerous offices throughout the U.S and U.K, touring and developing and maintaining one of today's hottest collectible lines must be exhausting. When you do finally get some time to yourself, what do you like to do?

N. Wiggins: I love motorcycling and going to museums on bright autumn days in New York. Somewhere along the way I would love to find a mate, build a magical home and fill it full of life and wonderful things!

Through The Eyes Of Martin Perry

CheckerBee Publishing was honored to have the opportunity to speak with Martin Perry about his outlook on Harmony Kingdom, creativity and life itself.

CheckerBee: At the age of 14, you headed toward a career in film, only to leave it several years later. Why is that?

M. Perry: I never considered a "career" in films. I was very young, my uncle was a producer and it was something to do. I was a boy up from the country suddenly hanging out with movie stars. I always felt very out of my depth and uncomfortable with such glamorous people. I still dislike the whole "movie" thing. I hardly ever watch a movie myself. I feel the same about television.

CheckerBee: Although I have read that you do not consider yourself an "artist," when did you first learn you that you had more of a creative urge that you needed to explore?

M. Perry: I don't consider myself an "artist" in the way that a painter or a sculptor would be considered artists. I do feel very creative and always have. I wrote a novel when I was fifteen years old and have started numerous novels since. I give up on them usually because I am so disappointed with my own ability. The actual words never get close to the vision. I wrote two hundred plus poems in the year preceding Noel Wiggins getting in touch with me. Needless to say I have written none since.

CheckerBee: You began your career by producing replicas of artwork. What did it feel like to create your first very own piece?

M. Perry: I had an almost physical sensation of pride. It was a tiny netsuke rabbit. When it was finished, I remember standing back and admiring it. I had turned a cup full of liquid "gunk" into something really quite beautiful.

CheckerBee: I read an account of a life-changing conscious moment of clarity that you experienced while hiking in the Himalayas. What can you tell us about that ?

M. Perry: We were at about 14,000 feet and it was raining heavily. I could suddenly hear a thunderous roaring above me. I had about five seconds to realize what was happening and find some protection. It was just luck that I was virtually standing beside a large rock outcrop. I flattened myself against it a moment before the first boulders began crashing over me. The noise was terrifying, some of the rocks were the size of houses. The whole of the side of the mountain above me was sliding down into the river thousands of feet below. And then it was over as quickly as it had begun. I sat shaking, trying to take it all in. It stopped raining and the sun came out. I couldn't help but think how lucky I was to be alive. Truly lucky and while thinking this, the sun was reflecting off a newly unearthed object in the debris just below me. I just let the light strike me for a while because I was too shaken to stand up, then I went over and picked it up, it was a crystal, about the size of an egg. I have chosen to imbue this crystal with magical properties. I still have it. There was nothing, per se, about this experience that was life-changing. It was just that in the day or two following, while still "high" on being alive, I did actually think that when I got home I should start making netsuke-like miniature boxes. In that sense it was life-changing.

CheckerBee: I believe that many people go through life without this experience. Have you had any other such experiences?

M. Perry: I have had many experiences of feeling "at one" with the universe. Without devaluing them in any way, I don't think they are particularly rare. You can almost become familiar with "at oneness." Various yoga or meditation techniques get you straight there, for me sitting quietly in a landscape, mountain or meadow can do the same. I mean, intellectually, we all know that we and the universe are one thing, after all, where is it exactly that you end and the universe begins? Feeling it does make you feel happy and humble. Mystical experiences, I think, are in another category. I don't think I have ever experienced anything that intense. They appear to be very extreme feelings of happiness and humility, enough to jiggle your genes around a bit. I do recall two "mental" experiences. One was a very strong "out of body" experience. It

occurred towards the end of a long lambing season. I had been living in a hut out in the fields above our village for about two and a half months. I don't think I slept more than two hours at a time since lambing had begun. This particular evening I had gone down to the village to see my wife. I remember lying down on the sofa and then suddenly I was floating up out of my body. I was still carrying on a conversation with Corinna, I think I even asked her if she could see me floating in the room. It went on for some time and I had time to calmly consider the situation. I think of it merely as a "novelty" probably brought on by exhaustion. When I was in my early twenties, a friend of mine said something to me that was so revelatory that my heart raced and my knees buckled. Neither he, nor anyone else in the room, thought his words were profound in any way. I won't tell you what he said, the words alone convey nothing of the significance that I chose to attach to them.

CheckerBee: How did you first feel when Noel Wiggins first contacted you about the many boxes he wanted to buy?

M. Perry: The first contact I had with Noel was by telephone. The conversation went something like this ..."Hi, my name's Noel Wiggins and I want to buy thousands of your boxes ..." "Well, Mr. Wiggins, I'm standing in my garden shed and I don't make thousands of boxes. Goodbye." He called me back later with a more subtle approach. I learned pretty quickly that Noel doesn't easily take no for an answer.

CheckerBee: What was it like when you first got together with Noel and Lisa?

M. Perry: I felt an immediate empathy with them. They were so young and enthusiastic about what they were doing, and so, it seemed, unorthodox in the way they went about running their business that I couldn't help but be drawn to them. I had a very strong sense, and still have, that there is between the three of us a blending of different personalities and talents where the total is certainly much greater than the sum of the parts. In the early months of Harmony Kingdom's formation, it really did seem as if everything was just falling into place in some kind of pre-destined way.

CheckerBee: Why do you believe people collect?

M. Perry: I think a lot about why people collect. The vast majority of HK collectors collect because they really like what we are doing, they derive an immense amount of pleasure from the whole experience. They enjoy the hunt, the socializing, the ownership of a piece or a collection. It has always been very difficult to know exactly what that is, but our particularly irreverent kind of humour must play a big part in it. Often there's a narrative to accompany the visual nuances and subtleties, often they are self-referring, there are the "secrets," there is the complexity of the carving and the quality of the carving. One collector once said to me, "your boxes tickle a part of my brain that nothing else touches." Maybe that's what it is, maybe that's all it is.

CheckerBee: I understand that Treasure Jests were first intended to be boxes that housed pieces of jewelry. What made you realize that they could be collectible themselves?

M. Perry: Yes, Noel and Lisa's first interest in the boxes was for that reason. The Harmony Ball Company was, at the time, primarily a jewelry company. They realized the potential in the boxes when people started asking if they could buy the box without the jewelry.

CheckerBee: Who have been the most influential people in your artistic career?

M. Perry: Peter Calvesbert without a doubt. We have enjoyed a very pleasant and relaxed working relationship for nearly ten years now. His contribution to the success of Harmony Kingdom cannot be overestimated. Between 1980 and 1990, the owner of the company making museum replicas was a major influence in my life. His name is Leigh Chapman. He taught me a lot of technical things about mold-making, materials and methods.

CheckerBee: How do you feel that the change in production location has affected the line?

M. Perry: The decision to do this was not arrived at lightly and in the end it was my personal decision. It was about the quality of my life. The business had grown at such a phenomenal rate and I was spending most of my time managing a factory that just got bigger and bigger every week. The pressure to produce was immense. I had not foreseen the impact this would have on my life. I never set out to manage a huge factory and neither did I want to bring in outsiders to run it for me, it would have changed the whole feel of the place. We now have a happy and efficient United Kingdom factory and a happy and efficient Chinese factory, and most importantly for me, I am spending more time doing what I enjoy most, being surrounded by sculptors creating new products. I know some people have been disappointed that we took this route, I hope they can understand the thinking behind it. They should always remember that the conception, the carving, the prototyping and the painting samples are all done by us in the U.K. just as they always have been.

CheckerBee: Do you believe that the close relationship between the artists is a contributing factor to the company's success?

M. Perry: I think it does make a big difference, but it's not some sort of clever company policy. It's just the way I am and it's built into the fabric of the business. It's not every company that survives to a size where the original "creative" people still hold the reins. Our artists certainly benefit from a close working relationship with the owners of the company and hence very much feel that they are right in the driving seat with us.

CheckerBee: What has been the most satisfying part about your work with Harmony Kingdom?

M. Perry: Really it's all one thing together. What has happened to me during the last four years should be set in the context of a man who had sort of semi-retired from the maelstrom of day to day life. I was without artistic or material ambition. I have enjoyed every minute of it. But part of that enjoyment has been because I have never had anything to lose and everything to gain. It is satisfying beyond measure to have helped create the "organism" known as Harmony Kingdom, and that is mostly about relationships with other people, relationships with my partners, with artists, with collectors, with factory managers, shop floor workers, retailers, reps; all of these people are a part of Harmony Kingdom.

CheckerBee: Is there one thought you could share with the huge group of devoted Harmony Kingdom fans?

M. Perry: After all you've put us through in the last four years, please don't stop collecting now!

CheckerBee: Can you ever see yourself stepping away from the world of art and going back to your life as a sheepherder or possibly even something else?

M. Perry: Not willingly. Of course the business may give me up. It has always been a worrying thought that a meteoric rise equals an equally meteoric fall. We will do our best to avoid that happening, but I guess we are in the hands of the collectors. If the collectors were to desert us, for whatever reason, then I suppose I will go back to my garden shed, write some poems and have some very happy memories.

A Day In the Life Of Lord Byron

Martin Perry continues to express his creative side with the story of Lord Byron of *Lord Byron's Harmony Garden*, released in chapters. But it's not the tale of the English Romantic poet. It's the continuing adventure of an intrepid ladybug who pines for love – and isn't afraid to search long and hard for it. A tale straight from the minds of Harmony Kingdom – a tale documented in the interiors of the boxes.

Harmony Garden is a charming world of flowers and color. And living all by himself inside the Rose is Lord Byron, manager of the Hydrangea Factory where he appropriately, makes flower boxes! But our hero's life isn't all work. Lord Byron is a lover of golf, who puts in many a game at the Rhododendron Country Club, and dreams of winning the Grand Golf Tournament at the Basket of Roses. An amateur astronomer, he also spends time at the Chrysanthemum Plant-a-tarium. Lord Byron is a practitioner of the arts too; he loves to view films at the Daisy Lounge and serenade himself on his pipe organ at the Peace Lily. But Lord Byron is a true Renaissance bug. He risks his life on a motorcycle at the Marsh Marigold Wall of Doom and keeps in shape by lifting 100 mustard seeds (or so he says) at the Hyacinth Gym. Quite a full life for a ladybug of independent means!

But Lord Byron isn't completely happy. After all, what good is a busy life without somebody with whom to share it? He doesn't have much luck finding love at the Snow Drop, and his only courting call at the Morning Glory leaves him rejected. But the Sunflower reveals a powerful message of hope to him: "Go round and round and upside down." Lord Byron takes this to mean that love is not to be found in this garden, and he sets out to find his soulmate.

Lord Byron decides to journey by sea at the Double Red Rose

Crossroads, and leaps into the water at the Snapdragon Cliffs. He then meets Roger, a hardened old wormer who introduces him to the joys – and perils – of fly fishing at the Gardenia Straits. After swimming to safety, Lord Byron finds an opportunity to speak his mind by debating Bergson the Blue Bug at the Forget Me Not Academy. The two gentlebugs then adjourn to the Iris Pub and Lord Byron joins Cricket Charlie in an impromptu jam session. And the music must be good, because Legs the caterpillar invites our hero back to her home at the Rose Bud! But sadly, their love is not yet to be. Lord Byron next shows off his athletic prowess with a soccer match against Gordy the Goalie Spider at the Begonia Field. It's not easy to beat a spider at soccer! But Lord Byron triumphs and gains a knighthood from the Queen Bee at the Peony Palace. After some time spent in the queen's Cactus Greenhouse, he remembers why he embarked on this trip to begin with and decides not to get side-tracked by his new honor. Following a farewell party at the Rose Party Room, Lord Byron makes his way to the Sunflower Station where Legs, now a butterfly, bids him godspeed.

Inspired by Don Quixote's words of wisdom, Lord Byron's story continues as he finds himself in the land of Tulips, where he repairs a dam and saves a windmill from destruction. Feeling the need to get some exercise, he then turns up skiing on the Alpine Flower Slopes, and then unwinding with a draft of beer at the Hops Bier Garten while flirting with Fraulein Emmet. After a few more beers, Lord Byron heads for the Pomegranate Hills, where the Olympics honor him by letting him be their official torch-bearer! He makes friends with the Italian team, who invite him back to their Hot Pepper Hideaway.

But Lord Byron won't bow down to their padrón, and barely manages to escape without getting his legs – all 6 of them – broken. On his way to Venice, Lord Byron meets Legs. Their date of boating on the Marigold Canal turns our hero's soul toward the art world. So he takes some time out to paint at the Sunflower Studio. He later boards Gill the Deep Sea Charter and sets sail for parts unknown.

Since finding love is proving difficult, our hero decides to embark on a quest for all things spiritual. His first stop is the Lemon Souk of Morocco, where he beats a local rug merchant at Parcheesi. His skill impresses the locals, and the Bedouin Locusts invite him on an expedition to the pyramids inside the Egyptian Rose – where he uncovers the tomb of the mighty ant king Tutanthamen! After viewing the king's amazing treasures, Lord Byron goes to Israel to ponder the Wailing Wall of Grapes – and studies The Cabala. Realizing he's onto something, he makes a pilgrimage to the Poppy Mosque of Istanbul, where he meets the TarantAllah while reciting from The Koran. Craving a deeper understanding of life, Lord Byron treks to the Himalayas and meets with the Daflea Lama at his Lotus retreat and becomes a tantric master. But the meditation proves too much for him, and he stows away to Japan. At the Cherry Blossom teahouse, a Geishabug is there to capture his heart – almost. Lord Byron then pilots the Albatross Aircraft for parts unknown – at least until Harmony Kingdom releases chapter five! If you can't wait that long, take a look at "Byron & Bumbles" for a clue.

Little does Lord Byron know that a mysterious female ladybug has appropriated his Home Sweet Home back in the Rose Garden. She's done a little redecorating, changing Lord Byron's lonely bachelor pad into a charming home, complete with an art gallery! How will our intrepid seeker of love and knowledge react to these changes when he finally returns home?

What's New In Harmony Kingdom®

This section highlights the new Harmony Kingdom pieces for the new millennium. Along with this release is the debut of two new series: Mini Treasure Jests and a new line of Picturesque tiles. The releases also include Special Event Pieces, Royal Watch Exclusives and the charitable Wee Beasties. There are 58 exciting new pieces to date, however Harmony Kingdom is full of surprises and you never know what might appear on store shelves in the near future. The following pieces are listed in the order that they appear in the Value Guide.

Catch As Catch Can . . . A curious little creature has become trapped in his master's watering can: a nice surprise for whomever is next to water the garden.

The Good Race . . . "What's the hurry?" wonders this slow-going turtle. He's taking his time, for he knows patience is a virtue and it's not who wins, but that it is a "good race."

Moggy Bag . . . This kitty has found a little bit of Heaven in a purse. Can the finicky feline find something he wants, or is it just a hunt for adventure that he is looking for?

Pot Sticker . . . Is he coming or going? Looks like he's coming up – through the bottom of the pots. And it looks like he may just be around for a spell.

Trunk Call . . . With trunk held high, this elephant lets out a call of freedom. He feels compelled to remind himself, as well as his friends, how fortunate they are to be free of captivity.

Cookie's Jar . . . It's easy to see temptation at work here. This innocent tabby, who was simply minding his own business, has now become a victim of obvious circumstances.

PHOTO UNAVAILABLE

Fusspot . . . There's no need to straighten out this dog's quirky attitude. With wrinkles from head to toe, there's quite a bit of smooth singularity to this delightful dog.

PHOTO UNAVAILABLE

Ed's Safari III . . . These safari animals may just be a bit more wild than most. In the third "Ed's Safari," the bags are packed and it's off to the road again.

PHOTO UNAVAILABLE

Retired Racers . . . In association with Greyhound Rescue and Adoption, these creatures are racing toward an unknown destination, hoping to find well-deserved R & R.

Special Delivery . . . The famous bearer of good news is again delivering the miracle of life, also bringing a plethora of reminders of the excitement and necessities that come with it.

Clair de Lune . . . This voluptuous woman's lounging suggests the atmosphere at the Clair de Lune 2000 convention – the only time she will be available. She's also the first piece in her own series.

Clair's Cat . . . What's a lounging woman without a regal cat at her side? "Clair's Cat," donned in flashy jewels, is another piece for those who join the Clair de Lune festivities.

Bon Bon . . . This little drummer boy anxiously awaits Christmas morning while playing his instrument. Perhaps he's making sure St. Nick doesn't pass him by.

Pastille . . . Too excited to sleep, this little girl is whispering her hopes of Christmas delight to her best friend, Teddy Bear.

Harry . . . Haste makes waste, but not to this poised-for-action hare. Believing the tortoise does win sometimes, he's not about to let "The Good Race" go by.

Nell . . . Attention has never been a problem for this doleful-looking pooch. With the combination of sad eyes and a curious friend hiding under her ear, "Nell" is quite the regal beagle.

Ollie . . . Whooo couldn't resist this beautifully carved owl? With his eyes strikingly fixed on his prey, "Ollie" gives collectors a rare glimpse of his most instinctual form.

Squee . . . Dolphins dance freely through untame waters. Capturing their grace and beauty, this piece introduces the enchanting world under the sea.

Tarka . . . Time has no problem passing this otter by, and he has no problem allowing it. What could be better than munching on lunch while floating out to sea?

Waddles . . . This majestic beauty waves her wings as in preparation for take-off. Or perhaps she's just carelessly waddling around for a while.

Pacer the Greyhound . . . "Pacer" is a retired racer, like those depicted in the box of the same name. Collectors electing to adopt "Pacer" will receive this *Wee Beastie.*

Manatee Wee Beastie . . . These manatee reside at the Columbus Zoo, and are the recipients of benefits of the *Zookeepers* adoption program.

Albatross . . . On another adventure, Lord Byron asks for help from an Albatross. Looking quite aerodynamic, he takes on a different appearance on the outside of the box, in a cool pair of shades.

Cherry Blossom . . . Lord Byron is wooed by fine music, dance and poetry in this teahouse. This bountiful bouquet is his last stop before continuing on his adventure to unknown destinations.

Egyptian Rose . . . Lord Byron and friends venture inside one of the great pyramids beneath the roses, and stumble upon "ant"cient treasures and remains.

Grapes . . . In Israel, Lord Byron becomes well-versed in The Cabala, and begins to learn the ways of the cosmos. This suits him just fine, as he has always had a longing for the mysteries of the sky.

Home Sweet Home . . . This little ladybug has found the home of her dreams in this bouquet of brightly colored flowers. The only problem is that it's Lord Byron's home.

Lemon . . . This stand is Lord Byron's first stop in his spiritual quest and it's hardly sour. Here, after beating a rug merchant in Parcheesi, the traveling ladybug begins his journey.

Lotus . . . Inside this bright yellow "Lotus" is where Lord Byron meets the Daflea Lama. Their meeting is beneficial, as it promises to further the ladybug's spiritual learnings.

Poppy . . . After his spiritual experience in the Grapes, Lord Byron turns to learning The Koran. Inside the "Poppy" mosque, he recites it for the higher beings.

Spring Bouquet . . . Spring has sprung in Harmony Garden and Lord Byron and his friends are celebrating. This limited edition of 5,000 pieces unveils our ladybug's dancing talents.

PHOTO UNAVAILABLE

Summer Bouquet . . . Just as quickly as Spring leaves, Summer appears. Lord Byron is so happy about it that he's called his mother. Could he be sending her a special wish?

PHOTO UNAVAILABLE

Bryon & Bumbles . . . Lord Byron keeps talking and his friend looks like he's hearing the same story over and over. It's also a limited friendship as only Royal Watch members can join their fishing trip.

Cow Town . . . Manatee glide through schools of fish and a mass of seaweed. Offered as a redemption piece for club members, it lends a vision for those who have never been close to sea life.

Field Day . . . These two critters are indeed having a "Field Day," nibbling and hiding. Indeed this mice are elusive, as they are only given to club members.

Lover's Leap . . . Personifying the game of Leap Frog, these leaping lovers hardly notice they've become part of another adventure – that of the 2000 Royal Watch Club Kits.

Merry-Go-Round . . . It's playtime as these three finned friends splash about. Perhaps they too are rejoicing in their participation in the 2000 Royal Watch Club Kits.

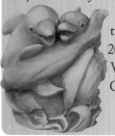

Silk Anniversary . . . This figurine is offered to collectors celebrating five years as a Royal Watch member. The piece also commemorates Peter Calvesbert and his wife, Andrea's fifth year of marriage.

PHOTO UNAVAILABLE

Wimberley Tales . . . As the third collection in the Picturesque line, these tiles tell the tale of a fictional town called Wimberley and its inhabitants.

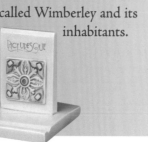

Club News

The Royal Watch™ Collector's Club

In response to the huge success of their collectible boxes, The Harmony Ball Company established The Royal Watch Collector's Club. The official club provides fans with the opportunity to keep up on all news and events relating to Harmony Kingdom, as well as offers special events in which these fans can meet other like-minded fans. The Royal Watch awards its members not only numerous benefits, but also a sense of really belonging to the Harmony Kingdom community.

The organization made its debut at the 1996 International Collectible Exposition in Secaucus, New Jersey. The collectors who joined the club received the "Garden Prince" pendant. With this pendant, the proud members could literally wear their love of the line. This tradition has continued and the club is growing by leaps and bounds as the years go by.

As the new millennium approaches, there is more exciting news for Harmony Kingdom collectors. First, 2000 welcomes the fifth anniversary of the Royal Watch.

For those who join or renew in 2000, their $40 membership fee entitles them to a year's subscription to *The Queen's Courier*, Harmony Kingdom's quarterly newsletter, which is not only informative but also highly entertaining. Club members will also receive certain exclusive pieces. The box figurines "Field Day," "Lover's Leap" and "Merry-Go-Round" are included in the 2000 Club Kit, and will make those who receive them the envy of the general collecting public. This kit also includes two coupons which can be redeemed for two more exclusive pieces: "Cow Town," a box figurine depicting manatee, which comes with an adopt-a-manatee offer, and "Byron & Bumbles," a multi-compartment box which features the intrepid Lord Byron fishing with his friend Bumbles. And to top it all off, members can also celebrate Peter Calvesbert's wedding anniversary with him by receiving the cake-topper figurine "Silk Anniversary."

Li'l Lords & Ladies Club

And the club isn't just for the kid at heart, but also for the kid too. Children 12 and under can now enjoy the exciting world of Harmony Kingdom by joining the Li'l Lords & Ladies Club. The membership is free and can be obtained when the child fills out the form found on the Facts Page of the www.harmonykingdom.com web site. Here kids can simply type in some personal information, including name, address and hobbies, and automatically become part of the club. Once a member, kids have the opportunity to learn fun information about Harmony Kingdom, play games, participate in contests and receive some great members only merchandise.

Local Collector Clubs

With the demand for Harmony Kingdom pieces rapidly increasing, collectors began forming their own local chapter clubs. In 1997, the first regional club was established in Portland, Oregon. It was called Harmony Northwest. Soon after, local clubs began forming all over the United States and the United Kingdom.

When an independent Harmony Kingdom club is formed, it has the opportunity to join with other clubs nationwide. The club can elect a delegate to the council of the House of Peers, a national organization which provides support to each independent collectors' club. Members of this council coordinate charity events, relay information from Harmony Kingdom to the local clubs and become involved in Harmony Kingdom decision-making.

Collectors looking for a club in their area should contact:

Harmony Ball Co.
ATTN: Royal Watch
232 Neilston Street
Columbus, OH 43215, USA

In the collectibles world, the retiring of a piece almost guarantees an increase in its value as it becomes less and less available on retail store shelves. For 1999, Harmony Kingdom bestowed this honor on 34 pieces. The retirements were held in April and September. In November, "Holy Roller" faced sudden death retirement.

Below is a list of these honored pieces with their issue year and code in parentheses.

SMALL TREASURE JESTS
❏ Antipasto (1998, TJAE)
❏ Baby Boomer (1998, TJKA)
❏ Catch A Lot (1998, TJWH4)
❏ Damnable Plot (1995, TJBV)
❏ Down Under (1997, TJPL)
❏ Faux Paw (1997, TJLI)
❏ Jersey Bells (1995, TJCO)
❏ School's Out (1993, TJFI)
❏ Too Much Of A Good Thing (1994, TJMC)
❏ Wishful Thinking (1998, TJTU2)

LARGE TREASURE JESTS
❏ Drake's Fancy (1990, TJLDU4)
❏ Journey Home (1991, TJLFI)
❏ One Step Ahead (1994, TJLTU)
❏ Quiet Waters (1990, TJLDU2)
❏ Tea For Two (1991, TJLWA)

EXTRA LARGE TREASURE JESTS
❏ Primordial Soup (1995, TJXXLTU)

TIMED EDITIONS
❏ Holy Roller (1999, TJSESA99)
❏ Love Nest (1998, TJSER98)
❏ Noel (1998, ANSE99T)

THE GARDEN PARTY

- ❏ Count Belfry (1997, TJZBA)
- ❏ Duc de Lyon (1997, TJZLI)
- ❏ Earl of Oswald (1997, TJZEL)
- ❏ Lord Busby (1997, TJZBE)
- ❏ Major Parker (1997, TJZMO)
- ❏ Marquis de Blanc (1997, TJZRA)

LORD BYRON'S HARMONY GARDEN

- ❏ Cranberry (1997, HGCR)
- ❏ Daisy (1997, HGDA)
- ❏ Gardenia (1998, HGGA)
- ❏ Hyacinth (1997, HGHY2)
- ❏ Hydrangea (1997, HGHY)
- ❏ Marsh Marigold (1997, HGMM)
- ❏ Rhododendron (1997, HGRH)
- ❏ Snow Drop (1997, HGSD)

Harmony Kingdom® Top Ten

This section showcases the ten most valuable Harmony Kingdom pieces as determined by their values on the secondary market.

1

Back Scratch

Small Treasure Jests
#CTJCA2
Issued 1993 – Retired 1995
Market Value: $4,500

2

Shark

The Elusive Few
#TJXXSH
Issued 1992 – Closed
Market Value: $2,500

3

Angel Baroque

The Elusive Few
#N/A
Issued 1996 – Retired 1997
Market Value: $2,250

PHOTO UNAVAILABLE

4

Panda

The Elusive Few
#TJXXPA
Issued 1992 – Closed
Market Value: $2,200

5

Who'd A Thought

Small Treasure Jests
#TJOW
Issued 1993 – Retired 1995
Market Value: $2,000

Ram

The Elusive Few
#TJXXRA
Issued 1993 – Closed
Market Value: $1,050

Chucky Pig

Special Event Piece
#XXXTJCP
Issued 1999 – Closed
Market Value: $750

Shoebill

The Elusive Few
#XXXTJSB
Issued 1995 – Closed
Market Value: $725

Sheep (Shaggy) Dog

The Elusive Few
#XXXTJSD
Issued 1993 – Closed
Market Value: $700

Let's Do Lunch

Small Treasure Jests
#TJVU
Issued 1994 – Retired 1995
Market Value: $660

Hallmarks

W hat do those symbols on the base and the lid mean? This is a way of telling you all about the history of that particular piece's creation – who carved it and when.

Most of the early pieces have no hallmarks, and it wasn't until 1993 that Calvesbert started carving his initials on them. A year later, pieces began appearing with a copyright.

Starting in 1995, four symbols began appearing on the box's exterior. A hallmark for the year of creation, the copyright, a clock face to show the month the piece was completed and Calvesbert's personal symbol – a staff and snake – began to appear. To show the year of production, a crown was stamped on the bottom of the base, which became known as the Production Hallmark stamp. Later that same year, Calvesbert's symbol was replaced with artist initials. Then in Autumn 1996, a label with production information began appearing on the piece's base. At that time, the Production Hallmark was moved to the underside of the box's lid. In 1997, an edition number replaced the carving month symbol and The Harmony Ball Company Logo was added.

Harmony Kingdom has had four symbols for the production year so far. The treble clef indicated 1995 or 1996. A heart was used in 1997, a five-pointed star in 1998 and a half-moon symbol in 1999. The Creation Hallmark has varied a bit. Pieces created in 1995 had an apple/bomb as homage to the Oklahoma City Tragedy and the 1996 pieces featured a diamond/coffin as a reminder of Martin Perry and wife Corinna's 1996 New Year's activities. The symbols for the next three years corresponded to those of the production year. The heart in 1997 to celebrate Lord Byron's introduction, a star in 1998 which Calvesbert carved into the first piece to be produced that year, "Sneak Preview," and the half moon in 1999 which celebrates the eve of the millennium.

How To Use Your Value Guide

1. Locate your piece in the Value Guide. Each piece appears alphabetically within its category, which are listed in the following order: *Mini Treasure Jests, Small Treasure Jests, Large Treasure Jests, Extra Large Treasure Jests, Series, Angelique, The Elusive Few, Harmony Circus, Special Event Pieces, Timed Editions, NetsUKe, The Garden Party, Other*

4   TJHE

40 Winks
P. Calvesbert • 51 x 39 x 41
Issued: 1992 • Retired: 1996
Market Value: $180

Harmony Kingdom Collectibles, Lord Byron's Harmony Garden, Royal Watch Collector's Club and *Picturesque.* Each piece is listed with artist, measurement in millimeters, issue year, status and variation if applicable. You can also use the handy Numerical Index beginning on page 169 and the Alphabetical Index beginning on page 171 to help you quickly find your piece.

2. Record both the original price that you paid and the current value of the piece in the corresponding boxes at the bottom of the page. Current pieces are listed with suggested retail price for their

Mini		
Date Purchased	Price Paid	Value
1.		
2.		
3.		
Small		
4. 3/93	35.00	180.00
	35.00	180.00
Totals		

Market Value. Retired and closed pieces for which a secondary market price has not been established are listed as "N/E." For those, write the price you paid in the "Value" column. The prices for variations that have significant value are listed as well. For a more detailed look at this pieces, please see the *Variations* section on page 153.

3. Calculate the value for each page by adding together all of the boxes in each column and recording it in the "Totals" section at the bottom of the box. Be sure to use a pencil so you can change the totals as your Harmony Kingdom collection grows!

4. Transfer the totals from each page to the "Total Value Of My Collection" worksheets located at the end of the Value Guide section.

5. Add the totals together to determine the overall value of your collection.

Treasure Jests®

The *Treasure Jests* collection makes up the majority of Harmony Kingdom's ingenious little boxes. With the 2000 introduction of *Mini Treasure Jests*, there's a size for every taste. More than 150 boxes make up the *Mini, Small, Large, Rather Large* and *Extra Large* groups, including six series of boxes within the collection: *Biblical, Black Box, Dueling Duet, Hi-Jinx, Paradoxicals* and *Zookeepers*.

Mini

1
New!

TJCA10

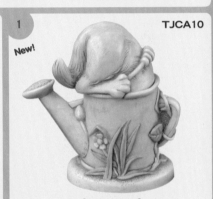

Catch As Catch Can
P. Calvesbert • 64 x 38 x 64
Issued: 2000 • Current
Market Value: $30

2
New!

TJTU3

The Good Race
P. Calvesbert • 38 x 57 x 38
Issued: 2000 • Current
Market Value: $30

Mini

Date Purchased	Price Paid	Value
1.		
2.		

Totals

1 TJCA9

New!

Moggy Bag
P. Calvesbert • 38 x 25 x 64
Issued: 2000 • Current
Market Value: $30

2 TJHE4

New!

Pot Sticker
P. Calvesbert • 45 x 45 x 64
Issued: 2000 • Current
Market Value: $30

3 TJEL3

New!

Trunk Call
P. Calvesbert • 38 x 38 x 64
Issued: 2000 • Current
Market Value: $30

Small

Mini

	Date Purchased	Price Paid	Value
1.			
2.			
3.			

Small

4.			

Totals

4 TJHE

40 Winks
P. Calvesbert • 51 x 39 x 41
Issued: 1992 • Retired: 1996
Market Value: $180

50

1 TJCA8

Algenon
P. Calvesbert • 45 x 55 x 83
Issued: 1998 • Current
Market Value: $45
Variation Value: $80 (Peter in bath)

2 TJME

All Angles Covered
P. Calvesbert • 50 x 50 x 57
Issued: 1994 • Current
Market Value: $35

3 TJRA

All Ears
P. Calvesbert • 61 x 33 x 44
Issued: 1993 • Retired: 1996
Market Value: $230

4 TJSN

All Tied Up
P. Calvesbert • 50 x 51 x 34
Issued: 1993 • Retired: 1996
Market Value: $200

5 TJAE

Antipasto
P. Calvesbert • 42 x 65 x 64
Issued: 1998 • Retired: 1999
Market Value: $45

Small

	Date Purchased	Price Paid	Value
1.			
2.			
3.			
4.			
5.			

Totals

Treasure Jests®

1 TJES

Aria Amorosa
P. Calvesbert • 49 x 72 x 75
Issued: 1998 • Retired: 1998
Market Value: $50

2 TJOC

At Arm's Length
P. Calvesbert • 42 x 41 x 58
Issued: 1993 • Retired: 1996
Market Value: $400

3 TJRA2

At The Hop
P. Calvesbert • 49 x 47 x 56
Issued: 1995 • Current
Market Value: $35

4 TJKA

Baby Boomer
P. Calvesbert • 61 x 61 x 71
Issued: 1998 • Retired: 1999
Market Value: $55

Small

	Date Purchased	Price Paid	Value
1.			
2.			
3.			
4.			
5.			

Totals

5 TJAR

Baby On Board
P. Calvesbert • 69 x 42 x 45
Issued: 1993 • Retired: 1997
Market Value: $48

Value Guide — Harmony Kingdom®

1   TJCA2

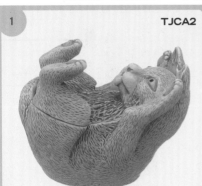

Back Scratch
P. Calvesbert • 59 x 34 x 46
Issued: 1993 • Retired: 1995
Market Value: $4,500

2   TJPA

Bamboozled
P. Calvesbert • 51 x 64 x 67
Issued: 1997 • Current
Market Value: $45

3   TJLB

Beak To Beak
P. Calvesbert • 56 x 41 x 57
Issued: 1995 • Retired: 1997
Market Value: $55

4   TJLEP99S

Bewear The Hare
(NALED Exclusive, LE-4,200)
D. Lawrence • 67 x 41 x 53
Issued: 1999 • Closed
Market Value: $48

5   TJSEG98F2

Boarding School
(GCC Exclusive)
P. Calvesbert • 69 x 49 x 50
Issued: 1998 • Closed
Market Value: $52

Small

	Date Purchased	Price Paid	Value
1.			
2.			
3.			
4.			
5.			

Totals

53

Treasure Jests®

1   TJCB2

Brean Sands
P. Calvesbert • 66 x 50 x 48
Issued: 1996 • Current
Market Value: $35
Variation Value: $400 (hand inside)

2   TJWH4

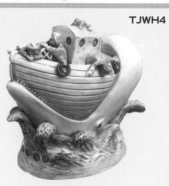

Catch A Lot
P. Calvesbert • 78 x 42 x 61
Issued: 1998 • Retired: 1999
Market Value: $45

3   TJCA6

Cat's Cradle
(NALED Exclusive, LE-1,000)
D. Lawrence • 63 x 61 x 63
Issued: 1997 • Closed
Market Value: $255

4   TJCA6B

Cat's Cradle Too
(NALED Exclusive, LE-1,000)
D. Lawrence • 65 x 62 x 62
Issued: 1997 • Closed
Market Value: $300

Small

	Date Purchased	Price Paid	Value
1.			
2.			
3.			
4.			
5.			

Totals

5   TJBB

Caw Of The Wild
P. Calvesbert • 89 x 57 x 64
Issued: 1999 • Current
Market Value: $45

1   **TJCH**

Changing Of The Guard
P. Calvesbert • 68 x 50 x 60
Issued: 1996 • Current
Market Value: $35

2   **TJHE3**

Close Shave
P. Calvesbert • 55 x 58 x 62
Issued: 1996 • Retired: 1998
Market Value: $50

3   **TJCA11**

New!

Cookie's Jar
P. Calvesbert • 51 x 51 x 64
Issued: 2000 • Current
Market Value: $45

4   **TJHICA**

Creature Comforts
(U.K. Exclusive)
M. Perry • 64 x 64 x 76
Issued: 1999 • Current
Market Value: N/A

5   **TJAL2**

Croc Pot
P. Calvesbert • 66 x 44 x 65
Issued: 1998 • Current
Market Value: $45

Small

	Date Purchased	Price Paid	Value
1.			
2.			
3.			
4.			
5.			

Totals

Treasure Jests®

1   TJBV

Damnable Plot
P. Calvesbert • 54 x 56 x 59
Issued: 1995 • Retired: 1999
Market Value: $36

2   TJPO

Day Dreamer
P. Calvesbert • 71 x 36 x 36
Issued: 1993 • Retired: 1996
Market Value: $525

3   TJHO3

Dead Ringer
P. Calvesbert • 59 x 71 x 63
Issued: 1999 • Current
Market Value: $45

4   TJWO

Den Mothers
P. Calvesbert • 51 x 57 x 51
Issued: 1995 • Retired: 1996
Market Value: $170

Small

	Date Purchased	Price Paid	Value
1.			
2.			
3.			
4.			
5.			

Totals

5   TJCICA

Disorderly Eating
(U.K. Exclusive)
M. Perry • 76 x 70 x 76
Issued: 1999 • Current
Market Value: N/A

Value Guide — Harmony Kingdom®

1   **TJHO**

Dog Days
P. Calvesbert • 59 x 49 x 56
Issued: 1994 • Current
Market Value: $35

2   **TJPL**

Down Under
P. Calvesbert • 54 x 53 x 56
Issued: 1997 • Retired: 1999
Market Value: $44

3   **TJZE**

Driver's Seat
P. Calvesbert • 40 x 62 x 80
Issued: 1997 • Current
Market Value: $45

4   **TJSA**

Ed's Safari
P. Calvesbert • 55 x 54 x 53
Issued: 1995 • Current
Market Value: $35

5   **TJSA2**

Ed's Safari II
P. Calvesbert • 76 x 51 x 64
Issued: 1998 • Current
Market Value: $45

Small

	Date Purchased	Price Paid	Value
1.			
2.			
3.			
4.			
5.			

Totals

Treasure Jests®

1 — TJSA3

New!

Ed's Safari III
P. Calvesbert • N/A
Issued: 2000 • Current
Market Value: $45

2 — TJKO

Family Tree
P. Calvesbert • 56 x 55 x 61
Issued: 1994 • Current
Market Value: $35

3 — TJLI

Faux Paw
P. Calvesbert • 62 x 65 x 59
Issued: 1997 • Retired: 1999
Market Value: $50

4 — TJSK

Foul Play
P. Calvesbert • 57 x 64 x 64
Issued: 1999 • Current
Market Value: $45

Small

Date Purchased	Price Paid	Value
1.		
2.		
3.		
4.		
5.		

Totals

5 — TJGI

Friends In High Places
P. Calvesbert • 55 x 45 x 87
Issued: 1997 • Current
Market Value: $45

1   TJCA3

Fur Ball
P. Calvesbert • 54 x 55 x 61
Issued: 1995 • Current
Market Value: $35

2   TJHO4

New!

PHOTO UNAVAILABLE

Fusspot
P. Calvesbert • 45 x 64 x 64
Issued: 2000 • Current
Market Value: $45

3   TJBP

The Great Escape
P. Calvesbert • 76 x 57 x 57
Issued: 1999 • Current
Market Value: $45

4   TJAA

Group Therapy
P. Calvesbert • 46 x 54 x 72
Issued: 1994 • Retired: 1996
Market Value: $265

5   TJPI

Hammin' It Up
P. Calvesbert • 47 x 46 x 40
Issued: 1993 • Retired: 1996
Market Value: $120

Small

	Date Purchased	Price Paid	Value
1.			
2.			
3.			
4.			
5.			

Totals

Treasure Jests®

1   TJLEP99F

Harmony Bull
(NALED Exclusive, LE-5,600)
P. Calvesbert • 76 x 51 x 44
Issued: 1999 • Closed
Market Value: $55

2   TJPI2

Hog Heaven
P. Calvesbert • 70 x 50 x 64
Issued: 1996 • Current
Market Value: $35

3   TJSE

Horse Play
P. Calvesbert • 47 x 46 x 69
Issued: 1995 • Retired: 1996
Market Value: $400

4   TJPU

In Fine Feather
P. Calvesbert • 58 x 57 x 73
Issued: 1997 • Current
Market Value: $45

Small

	Date Purchased	Price Paid	Value
1.			
2.			
3.			
4.			
5.			

Totals

5   TJMO

Inside Joke
P. Calvesbert • 54 x 45 x 58
Issued: 1994 • Current
Market Value: $35

1 TJHI

It's A Fine Day
P. Calvesbert • 61 x 33 x 48 or 59 x 33 x 47
Issued: 1993 • Retired: 1996
Market Value: $330

2 TJCO

Jersey Belles
P. Calvesbert • 56 x 54 x 54
Issued: 1995 • Retired: 1999
Market Value: $40

3 TJLEW99S

Jewels Of The Wild
**(Wild Birds Unlimited Exclusive,
LE-5,000)**
D. Lawrence • 98 x 88 x 118
Issued: 1999 • Closed
Market Value: $75

4 TJWH

Jonah's Hideaway
P. Calvesbert • 55 x 33 x 44
Issued: 1993 • Retired: 1996
Market Value: $275

Small

	Date Purchased	Price Paid	Value
1.			
2.			
3.			
4.			

Totals

Treasure Jests®

1 TJSEP98F

Kitty's Kipper
(NALED Exclusive, LE-5,600)
D. Lawrence • 60 x 60 x 45
Issued: 1998 • Closed
Market Value: $65

2 TJBD

The Last Laugh
P. Calvesbert • 73 x 59 x 92
Issued: 1999 • Current
Market Value: $45

3 TJVU

Let's Do Lunch
P. Calvesbert • 46 x 40 x 46
Issued: 1994 • Retired: 1995
Market Value: $660

4 TJEA

Liberty And Justice
P. Calvesbert • 64 x 45 x 80
Issued: 1996 • Current
Market Value: $45

Small

	Date Purchased	Price Paid	Value
1.			
2.			
3.			
4.			
5.			

Totals

5 TJBE

Life's A Picnic
P. Calvesbert • 50 x 57 x 50
Issued: 1995 • Retired: 1998
Market Value: $45

1 TJWA

Love Seat
P. Calvesbert • 58 x 43 x 57
Issued: 1994 • Retired: 1997
Market Value: $50

2 TJCA4

Major's Mousers
P. Calvesbert • 73 x 72 x 78
Issued: 1995 • Retired: 1997
Market Value: $110

3 TJFR3

Menage A Trois
P. Calvesbert • 57 x 45 x 71
Issued: 1998 • Current
Market Value: $45

4 TJBO

Mud Bath
P. Calvesbert • 73 x 46 x 54
Issued: 1995 • Retired: 1997
Market Value: $110

5 TJPB

Murphy's Last Stand
P. Calvesbert • 60 x 49 x 62
Issued: 1997 • Retired: 1997
Market Value: $65

Small

Date Purchased	Price Paid	Value
1.		
2.		
3.		
4.		
5.		

Totals

Value Guide — Harmony Kingdom®

1   TJRF

Neighborhood Watch
P. Calvesbert • 45 x 46 x 57
Issued: 1994 • Retired: 1997
Market Value: $85

2   TJHO2

Nic Nac Paddy Whack
P. Calvesbert • 62 x 50 x 67
Issued: 1996 • Current
Market Value: $45
Variation Value: $430 (bright colors)

3   TJTI

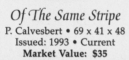

Of The Same Stripe
P. Calvesbert • 69 x 41 x 48
Issued: 1993 • Current
Market Value: $35

4   TJCM

Package Tour
P. Calvesbert • 55 x 52 x 67
Issued: 1999 • Current
Market Value: $45

Small

	Date Purchased	Price Paid	Value
1.			
2.			
3.			
4.			
5.			
	Totals		

5   TJSEP98S

Peace Offering
(NALED Exclusive, LE-4,200)
D. Lawrence • 52 x 54 x 63
Issued: 1998 • Closed
Market Value: $65

Value Guide — Harmony Kingdom®

1   TJWO2

Peace Summit
P. Calvesbert • 69 X 50 x 76
Issued: 1999 • Current
Market Value: $45

2   TJBM

Pecking Order
P. Calvesbert • 71 X 66 X 52
Issued: 1999 • Current
Market Value: $45

3   TJLEC99F

Pet Parade
(set/2, Parade Of Gifts Exclusive,
LE-5,000)
D. Lawrence
29 x 25 x 52 (cat) / 26 x 35 x 48 (dog)
Issued: 1999 • Closed
Market Value: N/E

4   TJTB

Petty Teddies
P. Calvesbert • 64 x 58 x 69
Issued: 1999 • Current
Market Value: $45
Variation Value: N/E ("Perished Teddies")

5   TJMA2

Photo Finish
P. Calvesbert • 83 x 45 x 70
Issued: 1997 • Current
Market Value: $45

Small

	Date Purchased	Price Paid	Value
1.			
2.			
3.			
4.			
5.			

Totals

Treasure Jests®

1   TJLEPA

Pieces Of Eight
(LE-5,000)
D. Lawrence • 85 x 73 x 109
Issued: 1998 • Closed
Market Value: $170

2   TJFL

Pink Paradise
P. Calvesbert • 60 x 59 x 74
Issued: 1996 • Current
Market Value: $35
Variation Value: $250 (untinted beaks)

3   TJFI2

Play School
P. Calvesbert • 58 x 42 x 43
Issued: 1994 • Retired: 1998
Market Value: $50

4   TJFR

Princely Thoughts
P. Calvesbert • 59 x 44 x 31
Issued: 1992 • Retired: 1996
Market Value: $140

Small

Date Purchased	Price Paid	Value
1.		
2.		
3.		
4.		
5.		

Totals

5   TJTO

Puddle Huddle
P. Calvesbert • 67 x 67 x 47
Issued: 1995 • Current
Market Value: $35

Value Guide — Harmony Kingdom®

1   TJCA

Purrfect Friends
P. Calvesbert • 52 x 55 x 50
Issued: 1994 • Current
Market Value: $35

2   TJSEG98F

Queen's Counsel
(GCC Exclusive)
P. Calvesbert • 51 x 51 x 63
Issued: 1998 • Closed
Market Value: $60

3   TJEL

Reminiscence
P. Calvesbert • 39 x 60 x 49
Issued: 1993 • Retired: 1996
Market Value: $240

4   TJRC

Rocky's Raiders
P. Calvesbert • 60 x 57 x 61
Issued: 1998 • Current
Market Value: $45

5   TJCA5

Rumble Seat
P. Calvesbert • 66 x 61 x 72
Issued: 1996 • Current
Market Value: $45

Small

	Date Purchased	Price Paid	Value
1.			
2.	2/14/02		
3.			
4.			
5.			

Totals

Treasure Jests®

1 — TJFI

School's Out
P. Calvesbert • 59 x 37 x 56
Issued: 1993 • Retired: 1999
Market Value: $38
Variation Value: $280 (no rocks)

2 — TJTU

Shell Game
P. Calvesbert • 47 x 57 x 52
Issued: 1993 • Current
Market Value: $35

3 — TJCB

Side Steppin'
M. Perry • 71 x 50 x 21
Issued: 1993 • Retired: 1996
Market Value: $125

4 — TJLE

Sleepy Hollow
P. Calvesbert • 64 x 47 x 48
Issued: 1997 • Current
Market Value: $35

5 — TJST

New!

Special Delivery
D. Lawrence • 76 x 51 x 89
Issued: 2000 • Current
Market Value: $45

Small

	Date Purchased	Price Paid	Value
1.			
2.			
3.			
4.			
5.			

Totals

68

Value Guide — Harmony Kingdom®

1   TJWH3

Splashdown
P. Calvesbert • 69 x 54 x 78
Issued: 1997 • Current
Market Value: $45

2   TJDO

Sunday Swim
P. Calvesbert • 47 x 63 x 53
Issued: 1994 • Current
Market Value: $35

3   TJAL

Swamp Song
P. Calvesbert • 46 x 46 x 58
Issued: 1993 • Retired: 1997
Market Value: $45

4   TJHU

Sweet Serenade
P. Calvesbert • 66 x 49 x 54
Issued: 1995 • Current
Market Value: $35

5   TJBI

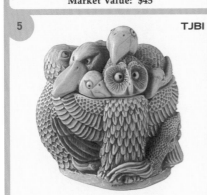

Teacher's Pet
P. Calvesbert • 52 x 42 x 56
Issued: 1994 • Retired: 1997
Market Value: $88

Small

	Date Purchased	Price Paid	Value
1.			
2.			
3.			
4.			
5.			

Totals

1   TJSH

Tin Cat
P. Calvesbert • 56 x 57 x 62
Issued: 1996 • Retired: 1998
Market Value: $55

2   TJFR2

Tongue And Cheek
P. Calvesbert • 50 x 50 x 50
Issued: 1994 • Current
Market Value: $35

3   TJCA7

Tony's Tabbies
P. Calvesbert • 52 x 63 x 79
Issued: 1997 • Current
Market Value: $45

4   TJMC

Too Much Of A Good Thing
P. Calvesbert • 48 x 48 x 58
Issued: 1994 • Retired: 1999
Market Value: $36

Small

	Date Purchased	Price Paid	Value
1.			
2.			
3.			
4.			
5.			

Totals

5   TJOR

Top Banana
P. Calvesbert • 45 x 55 x 51
Issued: 1993 • Retired: 1996
Market Value: $225

Value Guide — Harmony Kingdom®

1   TJEL2

Trumpeters' Ball
P. Calvesbert • 65 x 60 x 66
Issued: 1996 • Current
Market Value: $45

2   TJCR

Trunk Show
P. Calvesbert • 44 x 45 x 64
Issued: 1993 • Retired: 1996
Market Value: $210

3   TJBR

Turdus Felidae
P. Calvesbert • 49 x 55 x 89
Issued: 1999 • Current
Market Value: $45

4   TJMA

Unbridled & Groomed
P. Calvesbert • 60 x 63 x 52
Issued: 1995 • Retired: 1998
Market Value: $45

Small

	Date Purchased	Price Paid	Value
1.			
2.			
3.			
4.			

Totals

Treasure Jests®

1 TJPE

Unexpected Arrival
P. Calvesbert • 51 x 46 x 35
Issued: 1994 • Current
Market Value: $35

2 TJHE2

Untouchable
P. Calvesbert • 60 x 36 x 40
Issued: 1994 • Retired: 1995
Market Value: $350

3 TJWH2

Whale Of A Time
P. Calvesbert • 60 x 49 x 64
Issued: 1997 • Retired: 1998
Market Value: $52

4 TJPB2

When Nature Calls
P. Calvesbert • 68 x 59 x 50
Issued: 1999 • Current
Market Value: $45

Small

	Date Purchased	Price Paid	Value
1.			
2.			
3.			
4.			
5.			

Totals

5 TJOW

Who'd A Thought
M. Perry • 58 x 43 x 40
Issued: 1993 • Retired: 1995
Market Value: $2,000

Value Guide — Harmony Kingdom®

1   TJOW2

Wise Guys
P. Calvesbert • 55 x 54 x 52
Issued: 1995 • Current
Market Value: $35

2   TJTU2

Wishful Thinking
P. Calvesbert • 42 x 60 x 74
Issued: 1998 • Retired: 1999
Market Value: $75
Variation Value:
$80 (with full screw)
$60 (with partial screw)◄

3   TJLFR

Large

Awaiting A Kiss
P. Calvesbert • 110 x 79 x 57
Issued: 1991 • Current
Market Value: $55

4   TJLDU4

Drake's Fancy
P. Calvesbert • 107 x 56 x 64
Issued: 1990 • Retired: 1999
Market Value: $55

Small

	Date Purchased	Price Paid	Value
1.			
2.	9/01		

Large

3.			
4.			

Totals

73

Treasure Jests®

1 — TJLPE

Holding Court
P. Calvesbert • 135 x 102 x 81
Issued: 1995 • Current
Market Value: $55

2 — TJLRH

Horn A' Plenty
P. Calvesbert • 131 x 74 x 79
Issued: 1991 • Retired: 1997
Market Value: $70

3 — TJLFI

Journey Home
P. Calvesbert • 125 x 70 x 70
Issued: 1991 • Retired: 1999
Market Value: $55

4 — TJLDU3

Keeping Current
P. Calvesbert • 112 x 60 x 81
Issued: 1990 • Retired: 1998
Market Value: $52

Large

	Date Purchased	Price Paid	Value
1.			
2.			
3.			
4.			
5.			

Totals

5 — TJLEWH

Killing Time
(LE-3,600)
D. Lawrence • 144 x 94 x 94
Issued: 1997 • Closed
Market Value: $170
Variation Value: $240 (yellow sand)

Value Guide — Harmony Kingdom®

1   TJLDO

On A Roll
P. Calvesbert • 117 x 60 x 83
Issued: 1992 • Current
Market Value: $55

2   TJLTU

One Step Ahead
P. Calvesbert • 108 x 66 x 56
Issued: 1994 • Retired: 1999
Market Value: $58

3   TJLPI

Pen Pals
P. Calvesbert • 103 x 73 x 76
Issued: 1991 • Current
Market Value: $55

4   TJLDU

Pondering
P. Calvesbert • 115 x 56 x 68
Issued: 1990 • Retired: 1997
Market Value:
$155 (with interior egg)
$100 (without interior egg)

5   TJLTI

Pride And Joy
P. Calvesbert • 142 x 72 x 89
Issued: 1993 • Retired: 1998
Market Value: $60

Large

Date Purchased	Price Paid	Value
1.		
2.		
3.		
4.		
5.		

Totals

75

Treasure Jests®

1 · TJLDU2

Quiet Waters
P. Calvesbert • 101 x 57 x 63
Issued: 1990 • Retired: 1999
Market Value: $65

2 · TJLWO

Standing Guard
P. Calvesbert • 123 x 53 x 93
Issued: 1993 • Retired: 1997
Market Value: $120

3 · TJLCB

Step Aside
M. Perry • 141 x 88 x 50
Issued: 1993 • Current
Market Value: $55

4 · TJLHI

Straight From The Hip
P. Calvesbert • 130 x 86 x 73
Issued: 1991 • Current
Market Value: $55

Large

Date Purchased	Price Paid	Value
1.		
2.		
3.		
4.		
5.		

Totals

5 · TJLHE

Sunnyside Up
P. Calvesbert • 92 x 72 x 55
Issued: 1991 • Current
Market Value: $55

1 TJLFH

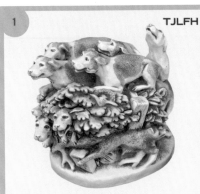

Tally Ho!
D. Lawrence • 98 x 85 x 73
Issued: 1999 • Current
Market Value: $65

2 TJLWA

Tea For Two
P. Calvesbert • 93 x 73 x 80
Issued: 1991 • Retired: 1999
Market Value: $60

3 TJLMA

Terra Incognita
D. Lawrence • 115 x 87 x 81
Issued: 1997 • Current
Market Value: $75

Rather Large

4 TJRLCA

Rather Large Friends
P. Calvesbert • 105 x 107 x 95
Issued: 1996 • Retired: 1998
Market Value: $75

Large

	Date Purchased	Price Paid	Value
1.			
2.			
3.			

Rather Large

4.		

Totals

77

Treasure Jests®

1 TJRLRA

Rather Large Hop
P. Calvesbert • 105 x 102 x 105
Issued: 1996 • Retired: 1998
Market Value: $65

2 TJRLTO

Rather Large Huddle
P. Calvesbert • 134 x 122 x 96
Issued: 1996 • Retired: 1998
Market Value: $65

3 TJRLSA

Rather Large Safari
P. Calvesbert • 111 x100 x 102
Issued: 1996 • Retired: 1998
Market Value: $75

Extra Large

Rather Large

	Date Purchased	Price Paid	Value
1.			
2.			
3.			

Extra Large

4.		

Totals

4 TJXXLTU

Primordial Soup
P. Calvesbert • 140 x 129 x 140
Issued: 1995 • Retired: 1999
Market Value: $160

1   TJLEBE

Unbearables
(LE-2,500)
P. Calvesbert • 176 x 129 x 150
Issued: 1995 • Closed
Market Value: $400

Biblical

2   TJLENO

Noah's Lark
(LE-5,000)
P. Calvesbert • 170 x 106 x 143
Issued: 1995 • Closed
Market Value: $455

3   TJLEGA

Original Kin
(LE-2,500)
P. Calvesbert • 130 x 128 x 137
Issued: 1997 • Closed
Market Value: $380

4   TJLESI

Sin City
(LE-5,000)
P. Calvesbert • 195 x 204 x 116
Issued: 1998 • Closed
Market Value: $600

Extra Large

Date Purchased	Price Paid	Value
1.		

Biblical

2.		
3.		
4.		

Totals

Black Boxes

1 TJBBVU

Have A Heart
(LE-3,600)
P. Calvesbert • 48 x 51 x 75
Issued: 1998 • Closed: 1998
Market Value: $210

2 TJBB99

Road Kill
(LE-5,000)
P. Calvesbert • 70 x 56 x 71
Issued: 1999 • Closed
Market Value: $185

Dueling Duet

3 TJLEG99F

Jump Shot
(GCC Exclusive, LE-3,600,)
M. Perry • 38 x 44 x 76
Issued: 1999 • Closed
Market Value: $52

Black Boxes

	Date Purchased	Price Paid	Value
1.			
2.			

Dueling Duet

3.		

Totals

1 TJLEG99S

Thin Ice
(GCC Exclusive, LE-6,000)
M. Perry • 48 x 54 x 76
Issued: 1999 • Closed
Market Value: $58

Hi-Jinx

2 TJXLPE

Antarctic Antics
P. Calvesbert • 97 x 98 x 100
Issued: 1994 • Retired: 1998
Market Value: $110

3 TJXLFO

Hold That Line
P. Calvesbert • 92 x 92 x 103
Issued: 1994 • Retired: 1998
Market Value: $110

Dueling Duet

	Date Purchased	Price Paid	Value
1.			

Hi-Jinx

2.			
3.			
		Totals	

81

Treasure Jests®

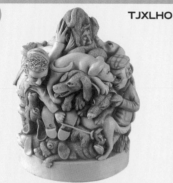

1   TJXLHO

Mad Dogs & Englishmen
P. Calvesbert • 91 x 86 x 111
Issued: 1994 • Retired: 1998
Market Value: $110

2   TJXLBA

Open Mike
P. Calvesbert • 98 x 95 x 88
Issued: 1995 • Retired: 1998
Market Value: $110

Paradoxicals

3   TJPPF

Paradise Found
P. Calvesbert • 52 x 53 x 56
Issued: 1995 • Retired: 1997
Market Value: $50

4   TJPPL

Paradise Lost
P. Calvesbert • 55 x 49 x 59
Issued: 1995 • Retired: 1998
Market Value: $52

Hi-Jinx

Date Purchased	Price Paid	Value
1.		
2.		

Paradoxicals

3.		
4.		

Totals

Zookeepers

1 TJLEMO

Family Reunion
(LE-7,200)
D. Lawrence • 83 x 83 x 105
Issued: 1998 • Closed
Market Value: $120

2 TJLEOW

Ivory Tower
(LE-7,200)
D. Lawrence • 88 x 88 x 113
Issued: 1998 • Closed
Market Value: $120

3 TJLEPO

Play Ball
(LE-7,200)
D. Lawrence • 92 x 92 x 104
Issued: 1998 • Closed
Market Value: $120

4 TJLEGR

New!

Retired Racers
D. Lawrence • 64 x 64 x 114
Issued: 2000 • Current
Market Value: $65

Zookeepers

	Date Purchased	Price Paid	Value
1.			
2.			
3.			
4.			

Totals

Angelique™ (side tab)

Angelique™

This exquisite line of boxes, created by artist David Lawrence was introduced as a series in June 1996. All but one, "Bon Chance," which is still available, were retired in April 1998. This five-box series is represented by three girl angels, a boy angel and a tooth fairy. The pieces' French names and elegant detail put the *Angelique* line in a class of its own.

1   ANBO

Bon Chance
D. Lawrence • 54 x 51 x 64
Issued: 1996 • Current
Market Value: $35

2   ANFL

Fleur-de-lis
D. Lawrence • 32 x 51 x 76
Issued: 1996 • Retired: 1998
Market Value: $50

Angelique™

Date Purchased	Price Paid	Value
1.		
2.		
3.		

Totals

3   ANGE

Gentil Homme
D. Lawrence • 36 x 56 x 65
Issued: 1996 • Retired: 1998
Market Value: $50

1 ANIN

Ingenue
D. Lawrence • 49 x 65 x 61
Issued: 1996 • Retired: 1998
Market Value: $38

2 ANJO

Joie De Vivre
D. Lawrence • 62 x 52 x 65
Issued: 1996 • Retired: 1998
Market Value: $42

The Elusive Few

These 10 boxes, three angels and seven animals, are very few and far between. That's because most of them were created prior to mid-1995, just before Harmony Kingdom made its way into the "collectible" world. The angel boxes were only released in the United Kingdom, and the animals were released in the United States in amounts of no more than 300. The majority of *The Elusive Few* do not have the inscriptions or hallmarks that have become so recognized in the later Harmony Kingdom pieces.

3 N/A

PHOTO UNAVAILABLE

Angel Baroque
D. Lawrence • N/A
Issued: 1996 • Retired: 1997
Market Value: $2,250

Angelique™

	Date Purchased	Price Paid	Value
1.			
2.			

The Elusive Few

3.		

Totals

The Elusive Few

1 TJXXPA

Panda
P. Calvesbert • 63 x 36 x 49
Issued: 1992 • Closed
Market Value: $2,200

2 TJXXRA

Ram
M. Perry • 65 x 40 x 41
Issued: 1993 • Closed
Market Value: $1,050

3 XXXTJRO

Rooster (Cockerel)
P. Calvesbert • 72 x 40 x 60
Issued: 1993 • Closed
Market Value: $600

4 N/A

PHOTO UNAVAILABLE

Rooster, Large
P. Calvesbert • 112 x 61 x 91
Issued: 1991 • Closed
Market Value: N/E

The Elusive Few

	Date Purchased	Price Paid	Value
1.			
2.			
3.			
4.			
5.			

Totals

5 TJXXSH

Shark
P. Calvesbert • 72 x 50 x 55
Issued: 1992 • Closed
Market Value: $2,500

1   XXXTJSD

Sheep (Shaggy) Dog
P. Calvesbert • 74 x 32 x 50
Issued: 1993 • Closed
Market Value: $700

2   XXXTJSB

Shoebill
P. Calvesbert • 54 x 36 x 65
Issued: 1995 • Closed
Market Value: $725

3   N/A

Teapot Angel I
D. Lawrence • 68 x 79 x 48
Issued: 1995 • Closed
Market Value: N/E

4   N/A

Teapot Angel II
D. Lawrence • 69 x 64 x 50
Issued: 1995 • Closed
Market Value: N/E

The Elusive Few

	Date Purchased	Price Paid	Value
1.			
2.			
3.			
4.			
Totals			

Harmony Circus™

The 22-piece *Harmony Circus* collection was David Lawrence's first major project with Harmony Kingdom. It was introduced in April 1996 and retired in July 1998. Harmony Circus fans had a chance to own some very special pieces, the limited editions "Bozini The Clown," "Madeline Of The High Wire" and "Numbered Circus Set" joined the circus.

1 HCAR

The Arch
D. Lawrence • 145 x 59 x 172
Issued: 1996 • Retired: 1998
Market Value: N/E

2 HCAU

The Audience
D. Lawrence • 109 x 80 x 112
Issued: 1996 • Retired: 1998
Market Value: $150

3 HCBA

Ball Brothers
D. Lawrence • 42 x 42 x 62
Issued: 1996 • Retired: 1998
Market Value: $35

Harmony Circus™

Date Purchased	Price Paid	Value
1.		
2.		
3.		
Totals		

Value Guide — Harmony Kingdom®

1 HCCL

Beppo And Barney The Clowns
D. Lawrence • 52 x 68 x 66
Issued: 1996 • Retired: 1998
Market Value: $35

2 HCZLECL

Bozini The Clown
(LE-10,000)
D. Lawrence • 38 x 32 x 39
Issued: 1998 • Closed
Market Value: $30

3 HCCR

Circus Ring
D. Lawrence • 91 x 25 x 19
Issued: 1996 • Retired: 1998
Market Value: N/E

4 HCCO

Clever Constantine
D. Lawrence • 50 x 41 x 71
Issued: 1996 • Retired: 1998
Market Value: $38

5 HCES

Great Escapo
D. Lawrence • 62 x 41 x 52
Issued: 1996 • Retired: 1998
Market Value: $35

Harmony Circus™

	Date Purchased	Price Paid	Value
1.			
2.			
3.			
4.			
5.			
		Totals	

1   HCHE

Henry The Human Cannonball
D. Lawrence • 46 x 53 x 58
Issued: 1996 • Retired: 1998
Market Value: $35

2   HCBE

Il Bendi
D. Lawrence • 77 x 57 x 47
Issued: 1996 • Retired: 1998
Market Value: $35

3   HCLI

Lionel Loveless
D. Lawrence • 54 x 50 x 67
Issued: 1996 • Retired: 1998
Market Value: $35

4   HCZLEMA

Madeline Of The High Wire
(LE-10,000)
D. Lawrence • 31 x 36 x 46
Issued: 1998 • Closed
Market Value: $40

Harmony Circus™

	Date Purchased	Price Paid	Value
1.			
2.			
3.			
4.	SEP '01		
5.			
	Totals		

5   HCTO

Magician's Top Hat
D. Lawrence • 33 x 41 x 64
Issued: 1996 • Retired: 1998
Market Value: $35

Value Guide — Harmony Kingdom®

1 HCSE

Mr. Sediment's Superior Victuals
D. Lawrence • 64 x 39 x 64
Issued: 1996 • Retired: 1998
Market Value: $35

2 HCSET

Numbered Circus Set
D. Lawrence • N/A
Issued: 1996 • Retired: 1998
Market Value: N/E

3 HCCA

Olde Time Carousel
D. Lawrence • 43 x 44 x 59
Issued: 1996 • Retired: 1998
Market Value: $40

4 HCPA

Pavareata
D. Lawrence • 52 x 56 x 62
Issued: 1996 • Retired: 1998
Market Value: $35

5 HCRI

The Ringmaster
D. Lawrence • 60 x 64 x 70
Issued: 1996 • Retired: 1998
Market Value: $35

Harmony Circus™

	Date Purchased	Price Paid	Value
1.			
2.			
3.			
4.			
5.			

Totals

Value Guide — Harmony Kingdom®

1 HCRO

Road Dogs
D. Lawrence • 40 x 60 x 67
Issued: 1996 • Retired: 1998
Market Value: $42

2 HCSU

Suave St. John
D. Lawrence • 52 x 3 x 65
Issued: 1996 • Retired: 1998
Market Value: $35

3 HCVL

Vlad The Impaler
D. Lawrence • 42 x 50 x 72
Issued: 1996 • Retired: 1998
Market Value: $42

4 HCWI

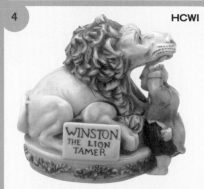

Winston The Lion Tamer
D. Lawrence • 47 x 74 x 68
Issued: 1996 • Retired: 1998
Market Value: $38

Harmony Circus™

Date Purchased	Price Paid	Value
1.		
2.		
3.		
4.		

Totals

Special Event Pieces

This group is made up of pieces produced for special occasions, such as collectibles conventions and open houses, as well as Harmony Kingdom gatherings like the Primordial Crooze and the Clair de Lune 2000 Convention. Pieces include boxes, figurines, pendants and even buttons.

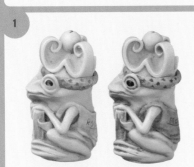

1996 Frog Pendant
P. Calvesbert • 29 x 28 x 48
Issued: 1996 • Closed
Market Value:
$350 (Rosemont, TJZFRR)
$500 (Secaucus, TJZFRS)

1997 Puffin Pin
P. Calvesbert • 57 x 51 x 10
Issued: 1997 • Closed
Market Value:
N/E (HK Puffin Pin, N/A)
$380 (Rosemont, XXXRO97P)

1997 Rose Pendant
D. Lawrence • 25 x 27 x 36
Issued: 1997 • Closed
Market Value:
$165 (Long Beach, XXXHGLB97)
$115 (Rosemont, XXXHGRO97)

Special Event Pieces

	Date Purchased	Price Paid	Value
1.			
2.			
3.			

Totals

1

1998 Angel Pendant
D. Lawrence • 35 x 26 x 46
Issued: 1998 • Closed
Market Value:
$88 (Edison, XXYE98Z)
N/E (Newark, N/A)
$70 (Rosemont, XXYRO98Z)
N/E (Stoneleigh, N/A)

2   XXYED98P

1998 Edison Lovebird Pin
P. Calvesbert • 43 x 48 x 19
Issued: 1998 • Closed
Market Value: N/E

3

1999 Lord Byron Pendant
M. Baldwin • 19 x 24 x 33
Issued: 1999 • Closed
Market Value:
N/E (Long Beach, XXYLB99Z)
N/E (Newark, N/A)
N/E (Rosemont, XXRO99Z)

4   TJROSE99

Camelot
M. Baldwin / P. Calvesbert • 84 x 45 x 62
Issued: 1999 • Closed
Market Value: NE

Special Event Pieces

	Date Purchased	Price Paid	Value
1.			
2.			
3.			
4.			
5.			

Totals

5   TJMINEVE

Cat's Meow
P. Calvesbert • 45 x 25 x 58
Issued: 1999 • Closed
Market Value: N/E

1   XXXTJCP

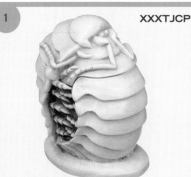

Chucky Pig
P. Calvesbert • 53 x 42 x 60
Issued: 1999 • Closed
Market Value: $750

2   N/A

New!

Clair de Lune
J. Bharucha • 76 x 89 x 89
To Be Issued: 2000
Market Value: $_____

3   N/A

New!

Clair de Lune Convention Special
N/A • N/A
To Be Issued: 2000
Market Value: $_____

4   N/A

Clair's Cat
P. Calvesbert • N/A
Issued: 1999 • Closed
Market Value: N/E

5   XXYTJCC

Crooze Cat
(Primordial Crooze Exclusive)
P. Calvesbert • 40 x 63 x 63
Issued: 1999 • Closed
Market Value: N/E

Special Event Pieces

	Date Purchased	Price Paid	Value
1.			
2.			
3.			
4.			
5.			
Totals			

95

Special Event Pieces

1   XXYTJZDR

Dragon Breath
D. Lawrence • 30 x 35 x 46
Issued: 1999 • Closed
Market Value: N/E

2   TJEVGO99

Gobblefest
P. Calvesbert • 64 x 70 x 76
Issued: 1999 • Closed
Market Value: $58

3   TJEVBE97

Oktobearfest
P. Calvesbert • 55 x 56 x 55
Issued: 1997 • Closed
Market Value: $55

4   N/A

Primordial Sloop
(Primordial Crooze Exclusive)
P. Calvesbert • 140 x 140 x 166
Issued: 1999 • Closed
Market Value: $300

Special Event Pieces

	Date Purchased	Price Paid	Value
1.			
2.			
3.			
4.			
	Totals		

1   TJEVPU98

Pumpkinfest
D. Lawrence • 55 x 56 x 55
Issued: 1998 • Closed
Market Value: $55

2   TJEVQJ99

Queen Of The Jungle
(Queen Empress Exclusive)
D. Lawrence • 86 x 76 x 89
Issued: 1999 • Closed
Market Value: N/E

3   TJICE98

Sneak Preview
(I.C.E. Exclusive)
P. Calvesbert • 79 x 73 x 69
Issued: 1998 • Closed
Market Value: $140

4   TJICE99

Swap 'n Sell
(I.C.E. Exclusive)
P. Calvesbert • 86 x 83 x 78
Issued: 1999 • Closed
Market Value: $85

5   TJROSE98

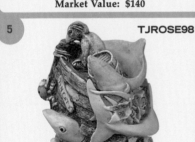

Tin Cat's Cruise
(Primordial Crooze Exclusive)
P. Calvesbert • 56 x 57 x 62
Issued: 1998 • Closed
Market Value: $345

Special Event Pieces

	Date Purchased	Price Paid	Value
1.			
2.			
3.			
4.			
5.			

Totals

1

XXXYTPPC

Tubbs Pin
P. Calvesbert • 38 x 6 x 51
Issued: 1999 • Closed
Market Value: N/E

Special Event Pieces

Date Purchased	Price Paid	Value

1.

Totals

Timed Editions

Timed Editions are eagerly awaited and collected by Harmony Kingdom fans. The collection is made up of *Holiday* and *Romance Annuals*, which have pieces added on a yearly basis, as well as the *Millennium* series, which for now only consists of one piece, "Y2hk." All of these celebratory pieces are released in a limited quantity, which makes them especially sought after.

Holiday Editions

1 TJZSE98

1998 Holiday Ornament Set
(set/4, LE-10,000)
M. Perry • 25 x 25 x 50 (each)
Issued: 1998 • Closed
Market Value: $100

2 ANSE00B

New!

Bon Bon
D. Lawrence • 45 x 57 x 76
Issued: 2000 • Current
Market Value: $35

Holiday Editions

	Date Purchased	Price Paid	Value
1.			
2.			
	Totals		

99

Timed Editions

1 TJ96AN

Bon Enfant
D. Lawrence • 80 x 35 x 41
Issued: 1996 • Retired: 1996
Market Value: $215
Variation Value:
$265 (green tunic)
$375 (orange tunic)

2 ANCE97

Celeste
D. Lawrence • 52 x 63 x 95
Issued: 1997 • Retired: 1997
Market Value: $60

3 TJAN

Chatelaine
D. Lawrence • 59 x 46 x 61
Issued: 1995 • Retired: 1995
Market Value: $300

4 TJSESA99

Holy Roller
P. Calvesbert • 80 x 97 x 58
Issued: 1999 • Retired: 1999
Market Value: N/E

Holiday Editions

	Date Purchased	Price Paid	Value
1.			
2.			
3.			
4.			
5.			

Totals

5 TJSESA98

Jingle Bell Rock
P. Calvesbert • 38 x 76 x 88
Issued: 1998 • Retired: 1998
Market Value: $60

Timed Editions

1 ANSE99C

Joyeaux
D. Lawrence • 64 x 71 x 85
Issued: 1999 • Retired: 1999
Market Value: $50

2 ANSE98

La Gardienne
D. Lawrence • 44 x 70 x 95
Issued: 1998 • Retired: 1998
Market Value: $55

3 TJSESA

Nick Of Time
P. Calvesbert • 50 x 81 x 61
Issued: 1996 • Retired: 1996
Market Value: $230

4 ANSE99T

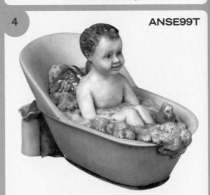

Noel
D. Lawrence • 53 x 100 x 66
Issued: 1999 • Retired: 1999
Market Value: $50

5 ANSE00G

New!

Pastille
D. Lawrence • 38 x 45 x 76
Issued: 2000 • Current
Market Value: $35

Holiday Editions

	Date Purchased	Price Paid	Value
1.			
2.			
3.			
4.			
5.			

Totals

Timed Editions

1   TJSESN99

Snowdonia Fields
M. Perry • 82 x 82 x 113
Issued: 1999 • Current
Market Value: $45

2   TJSESA97

Something's Gotta Give
P. Calvesbert • 51 x 50 x 82
Issued: 1997 • Retired: 1997
Market Value: $60

Millennium Series

3   TJSEY2K

Y2hk
M. Ricketts • 127 x 90 x 115
Issued: 1999 • Retired: 1999
Market Value: $175

Holiday Editions

	Date Purchased	Price Paid	Value
1.			
2.			

Millennium Series

	Date Purchased	Price Paid	Value
3.	DEC 2000		$175

Totals

Timed Editions

Romance Annuals

TJSER98

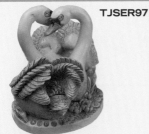

Love Nest
D. Lawrence • 66 x 66 x 85
Issued: 1998 • Retired: 1999
Market Value: $90

TJSER97

Pillow Talk
D. Lawrence • 123 x 70 x 83
Issued: 1997 • Retired: 1998
Market Value: $120
Variation Value:
$100 (red beaks/blue pillows)
N/E (yellow beaks/blue pillows)
$85 (yellow beaks/green pillows)

TJSER99

Tender Is The Night
M. Perry • 91 x 76 x 123
Issued: 1999 • Current
Market Value: $75

Romance Annuals

	Date Purchased	Price Paid	Value
1.			
2.			
3.			

Totals

NetsUKe™

This group of animal figurines is one of the new collections for 2000. Netsukes originated in Japan as carved toggles worn on Kimonos. Harmony Kingdom's version of these carvings was inspired by Martin Perry's work during his early days before Harmony Kingdom, creating replicas of netsukes for museums.

---

1 **TJNRA**

New!

Harry
P. Calvesbert • 25 x 64 x 38
Issued: 2000 • Current
Market Value: $20

---

2 **TJNHO**

New!

Nell
P. Calvesbert • 64 x 51 x 51
Issued: 2000 • Current
Market Value: $20

---

3 **TJNOW**

New!

Ollie
P. Calvesbert • 32 x 45 x 64
Issued: 2000 • Current
Market Value: $20

NetsUKe™

	Date Purchased	Price Paid	Value
1.			
2.	9/01		
3.			

Totals

NetsUKe™

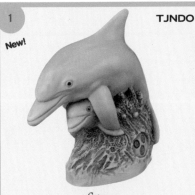

1 — TJNDO

New!

Squee
P. Calvesbert • 25 x 38 x 57
Issued: 2000 • Current
Market Value: $20

2 — TJNOT

New!

Tarka
P. Calvesbert • 38 x 57 x 38
Issued: 2000 • Current
Market Value: $20

3 — TJNDU

New!

Waddles
P. Calvesbert • 45 x 45 x 64
Issued: 2000 • Current
Market Value: $20

NetsUKe™

	Date Purchased	Price Paid	Value
1.			
2.	8/2001	$20	
3.			

Totals

The Garden Party™

This fashion-oriented grouping of pendants was introduced in January 1996, offering enthusiasts a stylish way to show their love for their collections. Since then, seven pendants have been retired (excluding event pendants), leaving only five still available.

1 **TJZPI**

Baroness Trotter
P. Calvesbert • 28 x 36 x 46
Issued: 1996 • Current
Market Value: $17.50

2 **TJZBA**

Count Belfry
D. Lawrence • 29 x 27 x 54
Issued: 1997 • Retired: 1999
Market Value: N/E

The Garden Party™

Date Purchased	Price Paid	Value
1.		
2.		
3.		

Totals

3 **TJZTU**

Courtiers At Rest
P. Calvesbert • 34 x 33 x 46
Issued: 1996 • Current
Market Value: $17.50

1 TJZLI

Duc De Lyon
D. Lawrence • 30 x 35 x 50
Issued: 1997 • Retired: 1999
Market Value: N/E

2 TJZEL

Earl Of Oswald
D. Lawrence • 31 x 34 x 47
Issued: 1997 • Retired: 1999
Market Value: N/E

3 TJZFR

Garden Prince
P. Calvesbert • 29 x 28 x 48
Issued: 1996 • Current
Market Value: $17.50

4 TJZCA

Ladies In Waiting
P. Calvesbert • 31 x 29 x 47
Issued: 1996 • Current
Market Value: $17.50

5 TJZBE

Lord Busby
D. Lawrence • 31 x 27 x 49
Issued: 1997 • Retired: 1999
Market Value: N/E

The Garden Party™

	Date Purchased	Price Paid	Value
1.			
2.			
3.			
4.			
5.			
Totals			

The Garden Party™

1 TJZMO

Major Parker
D. Lawrence • 29 x 33 x 48
Issued: 1997 • Retired: 1999
Market Value: N/E

2 TJZRA

Marquis De Blanc
D. Lawrence • 27 x 35 x 51
Issued: 1997 • Retired: 1999
Market Value: N/E

3 TJZFI

Royal Flotilla
P. Calvesbert • 36 x 25 x 50
Issued: 1996 • Retired: 1998
Market Value: N/E

4 TJZOW

Yeoman Of The Guard
P. Calvesbert • 26 x 25 x 30
Issued: 1996 • Current
Market Value: $17.50

The Garden Party™

	Date Purchased	Price Paid	Value
1.			
2.			
3.			
4.			

Totals

Other Harmony Kingdom® Collectibles

There are several other products that have come along which are just as creative and collectible: pewter pens, sterling pendants, a QVC exclusive pin, exclusive Disney Theme Park pieces and miniature figurine replicas of the *Zookeepers* pieces called *Wee Beasties*. Also, two limited edition teapots and a set of "Paint Your Own" figurines have been exclusively created for Harmony Kingdom by Cardew Designs.

1 WDWFABFIVE

Fab Five
(Disney Exclusive)
Disney Artist • 103 x 95 x 95
Issued: 1997 • Current
Market Value: N/A

2 WDWLIONKING

Lion King's Pride Rock
(Disney Exclusive)
Disney Artist • 108 x 106 x 101
Issued: 1998 • Current
Market Value: N/A

3 WDWPIN

Pinocchio's Great Adventure
(Disney Exclusive)
Disney Artist • 102 x 46 x 90
Issued: 1999 • Current
Market Value: N/A

Disney Exclusives

	Date Purchased	Price Paid	Value
1.			
2.			
3.			
		Totals	

Other Harmony Kingdom® Collectibles

1 **WDWPOOH**

Pooh And Friends
(Disney Exclusive)
Disney Artist • 77 x 78 x 78
Issued: 1997 • Current
Market Value: N/A

2 **WDWSNOWWHITE**

Snow White
(Disney Exclusive)
Disney Artist • 86 x 85 x 98
Issued: 1999 • Current
Market Value: N/A

3 **HKPY1**

Paint Your Own
P. Cardew / M. Perry • Various
Issued: 1999 • Current
Market Value: $35

4 **TJZLESSPI**

Disney Exclusives

	Date Purchased	Price Paid	Value
1.			
2.			

Paint Your Own

3.			

Pendants

4.			

Totals

Sterling Silver Baroness Trotter
Pendant (LE-5,000)
M. Perry • 13 x 15 x 28
Issued: 1999 • Closed
Market Value: N/E

1   TJZLESSFR

Sterling Silver Garden Prince
Pendant (LE-5,000)
M. Perry • 15 x 15 x 28
Issued: 1999 • Closed
Market Value: N/E

2   TJZLESSLB

Sterling Silver Lord Byron
Pendant (LE-5,000)
M. Perry • 10 x 15 x 29
Issued: 1999 • Closed
Market Value: N/E

3   HKPEN1

Scratching Post Pewter Pen
(LE-10,000)
P. Calvesbert • 13 x 15 x 145
Issued: 1997 • Closed
Market Value: $45

4   HKPEN2

Tabby Totem Pewter Pen
(LE-10,000)
P. Calvesbert • 10 x 10 x 143
Issued: 1997 • Closed
Market Value: $45

5   XXXYQVC

QVC Pin
(QVC Exclusive)
M. Baldwin • 38 x 6 x 51
Issued: 1999 • Closed
Market Value: N/E

Pendants		
Date Purchased	Price Paid	Value
1.		
2.		
Pens		
3.		
4.		
Pins		
5.		
Totals		

Other Harmony Kingdom® Collectibles

1 — HCLESER

Harmony Circus Serigraph
(LE-1,000)
D. Lawrence • 445 x 560
Issued: 1998 • Closed
Market Value: N/E

2 — HKTPLECB

Cracking Brew (LE-3,850)
P. Calvesbert / P. Cardew • 177 x 241 x 152
Issued: 1999 • Closed
Market Value: $170

3 — HKTPLET42

Yt42hk (LE-4,850)
P. Calvesbert / P. Cardew • 152 x 241 x 203
Issued: 1999 • Closed
Market Value: N/E

4 — XXXTJLEOW

Helen the Owl
D. Lawrence • 88 x 88 x 113
Issued: 1999 • Current
Market Value: $30-$40

5 — N/A

New!

Manatee Wee Beastie
D. Lawrence • N/A
Issued: 2000 • Current
Market Value: $30-$40

Prints

Date Purchased	Price Paid	Value
1.		

Teapots

2.		
3.		

Wee Beasties

4.		
5.		

Totals

1   XXYTJLEPO

Marty the Polar Bear
D. Lawrence • 25 x 19 x 32
Issued: 1999 • Current
Market Value: $30-$40

2   XXYTJLEGR

New!

Pacer the Greyhound
M. Perry • 19 x 32 x 45
Issued: 2000 • Current
Market Value: $30-$40

3   XXYRW99PE

Pip the Pelican
D. Lawrence • 45 x 38 x 51
Issued: 1999 • Current
Market Value: $30-$40

4   XXXTJLEMO

Zephry the Monkey
D. Lawrence • 83 x 83 x 105
Issued: 1999 • Current
Market Value: $30-$40

Wee Beasties

	Date Purchased	Price Paid	Value
1.			
2.			
3.			
4.			

Totals

Lord Byron's Harmony Garden®

These entertaining little boxes tell the story of the travels of a lady-bug named Lord Byron. On the outside of the boxes are flowers (with a few exceptions, like "Hot Pepper" and "Gill"), with Lord Byron on the inside. Each release is called a chapter, and so far, there are four, including limited editions and holiday bouquets. Every chapter reveals clues as to what will happen in the next, while the traveling hero's final destination remains a well-guarded secret.

Chapter One

1

HGCH

Chrysanthemum
M. Perry • 65 x 55 x 66
Issued: 1997 • Current
Market Value: $38.50

Chapter One

Date Purchased	Price Paid	Value
1.		
2.		

Totals

2

HGCR

Cranberry
M. Perry • 67 x 55 x 63
Issued: 1997 • Retired: 1999
Market Value: $50

Lord Byron's Harmony Garden®

1 — HGDA

Daisy
M. Perry • 58 x 52 x 55
Issued: 1997 • Retired: 1999
Market Value: $50

2 — HGHY2

Hyacinth
M. Perry • 62 x 55 x 67
Issued: 1997 • Retired: 1999
Market Value: $50

3 — HGHY

Hydrangea
M. Perry • 78 x 59 x 47
Issued: 1997 • Retired: 1999
Market Value: $50

4 — HGMM

Marsh Marigold
M. Perry • 58 x 62 x 67
Issued: 1997 • Retired: 1999
Market Value: $50

5 — HGMG

Morning Glory
M. Perry • 66 x 50 x 82
Issued: 1997 • Current
Market Value: $38.50

Chapter One

	Date Purchased	Price Paid	Value
1.			
2.			
3.			
4.			
5.			
Totals			

Lord Byron's Harmony Garden®

1   HGPL

Peace Lily
M. Perry • 53 x 47 x 72
Issued: 1997 • Current
Market Value: $38.50

2   HGRH

Rhododendron
M. Perry • 58 x 56 x 74
Issued: 1997 • Retired: 1999
Market Value: $50

3   HGLELR

Rose Basket
(LE-3,600)
M. Perry • 109 x 83 x 79
Issued: 1997 • Closed
Market Value: $160

4   HGLEOR

Single Orange Rose
(LE-3,600)
M. Perry • 48 x 52 x 53
Issued: 1997 • Closed
Market Value: $110

Chapter One

	Date Purchased	Price Paid	Value
1.			
2.			
3.			
4.			
5.			

Totals

5   HGLEPR

Single Pink Rose
(LE-3,600)
M. Perry • 48 x 52 x 53
Issued: 1997 • Closed
Market Value: $100

Value Guide — Harmony Kingdom®

1   HGLERR

Single Red Rose
(LE-3,600)
M. Perry • 48 x 52 x 53
Issued: 1997 • Closed
Market Value: $250

2   HGLEVR

Single Violet Rose
(LE-3,600)
M. Perry • 48 x 52 x 53
Issued: 1997 • Closed
Market Value: $110

3   HGLEWR

Single White Rose
(LE-3,600)
M. Perry • 48 x 52 x 53
Issued: 1997 • Closed
Market Value: $120

4   HGLEYR

Single Yellow Rose
(LE-3,600)
M. Perry • 48 x 52 x 53
Issued: 1997 • Closed
Market Value: $110

5   HGSD

Snow Drop
M. Perry • 49 x 43 x 68
Issued: 1997 • Retired: 1999
Market Value: $50

Chapter One

	Date Purchased	Price Paid	Value
1.			
2.			
3.			
4.			
5.			
	Totals		

Chapter Two

1 HGBE

Begonia
M. Perry • 61 x 65 x 77
Issued: 1998 • Current
Market Value: $45

2 HGCA

Cactus
M. Perry • 78 x 68 x 59
Issued: 1998 • Current
Market Value: $45

3 HGLEDPR

Double Pink Rose
(LE-5,000)
M. Perry • 87 x 65 x 53
Issued: 1998 • Closed
Market Value: $85

Chapter Two

	Date Purchased	Price Paid	Value
1.			
2.			
3.			
4.			

Totals

4 HGLEDRR

Double Red Rose
(LE-5,000)
M. Perry • 87 x 65 x 53
Issued: 1998 • Closed
Market Value: $85

1 HGLEDVR

Double Violet Rose
(LE-5,000)
M. Perry • 87 x 65 x 53
Issued: 1998 • Closed
Market Value: $85

2 HGLEDYR

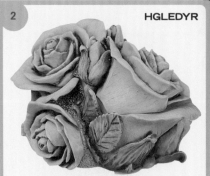

Double Yellow Rose
(LE-5,000)
M. Perry • 87 x 65 x 53
Issued: 1998 • Closed
Market Value: $85

3 HGFM

Forget Me Not
M. Perry • 75 x 67 x 57
Issued: 1998 • Current
Market Value: $45

4 HGGA

Gardenia
M. Perry • 77 x 63 x 60
Issued: 1998 • Retired: 1999
Market Value: N/E

5 HGIR

Iris
M. Perry • 58 x 46 x 79
Issued: 1998 • Current
Market Value: $45

Chapter Two

	Date Purchased	Price Paid	Value
1.			
2.			
3.			
4.			
5.			

Totals

119

Lord Byron's Harmony Garden®

1   HGPE

Peony
M. Perry • 70 x 67 x 77
Issued: 1998 • Current
Market Value: $45

2   HGRB

Rose Bud
M. Baldwin • 68 x 66 x 64
Issued: 1998 • Current
Market Value: $45

3   HGLELR2

Rose Party
(LE-5,000)
M. Perry • 87 x 84 x 94
Issued: 1998 • Closed
Market Value: $110

4   HGSN

Snapdragon
M. Perry • 65 x 60 x 77
Issued: 1998 • Current
Market Value: $45

Chapter Two

	Date Purchased	Price Paid	Value
1.			
2.			
3.			
4.			
5.			

Totals

5   HGLESR

Sterling Rose
(Queen Empress Exclusive, LE-1,000)
M. Perry • 48 x 51 x 41
Issued: 1998 • Closed
Market Value: $425

1   HGSU

Sunflower
M. Perry • 68 x 65 x 67
Issued: 1998 • Current
Market Value: $45

Chapter
Three

2   HG3AL

Alpine Flower
M. Baldwin • 80 x 72 x 74
Issued: 1999 • Current
Market Value: $45

3   HG3LEBQC

Christmas Bouquet
(LE-5,000)
M. Perry • 91 x 97 x 67
Issued: 1999 • Closed
Market Value: $80

4   HGLEDSR

Double Sterling Rose
(Queen Empress Exclusive, LE-1,500)
M. Perry • 82 x 60 x 48
Issued: 1999 • Closed
Market Value: N/E

Lord Byron's Harmony Garden®

Chapter Two

	Date Purchased	Price Paid	Value
1.			

Chapter Three

2.			
3.			
4.			

Totals

Lord Byron's Harmony Garden®

1   HG3LEBQE

Easter Bouquet
(LE-5,000)
S. Drackett • 91 x 97 x 67
Issued: 1999 • Closed
Market Value: $80

2   HG3GI

Gill
M. Baldwin • 92 x 65 x 58
Issued: 1999 • Current
Market Value: $45

3   HG3LEBQH

Halloween Bouquet
(LE-5,000)
M. Perry • 90 x 84 x 71
Issued: 1999 • Closed
Market Value: $80

4   HG3HO

Hops
M. Baldwin • 61 x 63 x 81
Issued: 1999 • Current
Market Value: $45

Chapter Three

	Date Purchased	Price Paid	Value
1.			
2.	12/01		
3.			
4.			
5.			
	Totals		

5   HG3HP

Hot Pepper
M. Baldwin • 83 x 80 x 83
Issued: 1999 • Current
Market Value: $45

1   HG3MA

Marigold
M. Baldwin • 72 x 74 x 75
Issued: 1999 • Current
Market Value: $45

2   HG3LEBQM

Mother's Day Bouquet
(LE-5,000)
S. Drackett • 88 x 91 x 97
Issued: 1999 • Closed
Market Value: $75

3   HG3OR

Orange
M. Baldwin • 90 x 78 x 70
Issued: 1999 • Current
Market Value: $45

4   HGLEC99S

Parade of Gifts
(Parade Of Gifts Exclusive, LE-5,000)
M. Perry • 83 x 84 x 63
Issued: 1999 • Closed
Market Value: N/E

5   HG3PO

Pomegranate
M. Baldwin • 92 x 80 x 66
Issued: 1999 • Current
Market Value: $45

Chapter Three

	Date Purchased	Price Paid	Value
1.			
2.			
3.			
4.			
5.			
	Totals		

Lord Byron's Harmony Garden®

Value Guide — Harmony Kingdom®

1   HG3SU

Sunflower II
M. Baldwin • 75 x 61 x 72
Issued: 1999 • Current
Market Value: $45

2   HG3TU

Tulip
M. Baldwin • 72 x 70 x 82
Issued: 1999 • Current
Market Value: $45

Chapter Four

3   HG4AL

New!

Albatross
M. Baldwin • 76 x 51 x 89
Issued: 2000 • Current
Market Value: $45

4   HG4CB

New!

Chapter Three

Date Purchased	Price Paid	Value
1.		
2.		

Chapter Four

3.		
4.		

Totals

Cherry Blossom
M. Baldwin • 70 x 64 x 76
Issued: 2000 • Current
Market Value: $45

1 — HG4ER

New!

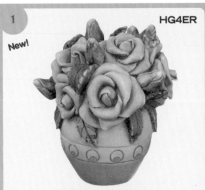

Egyptian Rose
M. Baldwin • 76 x 76 x 95
Issued: 2000 • Current
Market Value: $45

2 — HG4GR

New!

Grapes
M. Baldwin • 102 x 89 x 45
Issued: 2000 • Current
Market Value: $45

3 — HGLELR3

New!

Home Sweet Home
(LE-3,600)
M. Perry • 178 x 178 x 165
Issued: 2000 • Current
Market Value: $250

4 — HG4LE

New!

Lemon
M. Baldwin • 64 x 51 x 76
Issued: 2000 • Current
Market Value: $45

5 — HG4LO

New!

Lotus
M. Baldwin • 89 x 89 x 76
Issued: 2000 • Current
Market Value: $45

Chapter Four

	Date Purchased	Price Paid	Value
1.			
2.			
3.			
4.			
5.			
	Totals		

1 New! HG4PO

Poppy
M. Baldwin • 76 x 76 x 89
Issued: 2000 • Current
Market Value: $45

2 New! HG4LEBQSP

Spring Bouquet
(LE-5,000)
S. Drackett • 83 x 83 x 95
Issued: 2000 • Current
Market Value: $75

3 New! HG4LEBQSU

Summer Bouquet
(LE-5,000)
S. Drackett • 89 x 89 x 108
Issued: 2000 • Current
Market Value: $75

Chapter Four

Date Purchased	Price Paid	Value
1.		
2.		
3.		

Totals

Royal Watch™ Collector's Club

Since the Royal Watch™ Collector's Club was
introduced in 1995, members have received
special pieces. Some are gifts for becoming a member, while some are pieces that
you can purchase. Also, pieces are given
away at the collectibles conventions each
year to existing members, or those who
sign up at the event. Pieces include
boxes, pendants and a pewter pen.

1 RWIGK99

Royal Watch 1999 Club Kit
N/A • N/A
Issued: 1999 • Closed
Market Value: N/E

2 RWIGK00

New!

PHOTO
UNAVAILABLE

Royal Watch 2000 Club Kit
N/A • N/A
Issued: 2000 • Current
Market Value: $40

Members Only

Club Kits

	Date Purchased	Price Paid	Value
1.			
2.			

Totals

Royal Watch™ Collector's Club

Value Guide — Harmony Kingdom®

1   **RW98PEN**

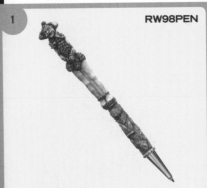

April's Fool Pewter Pen
P. Calvesbert • 10 x 10 x 143
Issued: 1998 • Closed
Market Value: N/E

2   **RW99SS**

Beneath the Ever Changing Seas
D. Lawrence • 74 x 52 x 71
Issued: 1999 • Closed
Market Value: N/E

3   **RW98PI**

Cat Pin
P. Calvesbert • 54 x 47 x 13
Issued: 1998 • Closed
Market Value: $22

4   **RW00MO**

New!

Field Day
S. Drackett • 51 x 51 x 51
Issued: 2000 • Current
Market Value: Membership Gift

Members Only

	Date Purchased	Price Paid	Value
1.			
2.			
3.			
4.			
5.			

Totals

5   **RW00FR**

New!

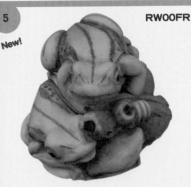

Lover's Leap
S. Drackett • 38 x 45 x 38
Issued: 2000 • Current
Market Value: Membership Gift

Value Guide — Harmony Kingdom®

1   RW00DO

New!

Merry-Go-Round
SD • 38 x 38 x 45
Issued: 2000 • Current
Market Value: Membership Gift

2   RW99PI

ROYAL WATCH

Murphy Pin
P. Calvesbert • 38 x 9 x 48
Issued: 1999 • Closed
Market Value: N/E

3   RW98MC

Mutton Chops
P. Calvesbert • 52 x 46 x 58
Issued: 1998 • Closed
Market Value: $42

4   RW96DL

Purrfect Fit
D. Lawrence • 75 x 59 x 66
Issued: 1996 • Closed
Market Value: $330

5   RW97DL

Sweet As A Summer's Kiss
D. Lawrence • 46 x 42 x 49
Issued: 1997 • Closed
Market Value: $60

Members Only

	Date Purchased	Price Paid	Value
1.			
2.			
3.			
4.			
5.			
Totals			

Value Guide — Harmony Kingdom®

1   RW97PC

Toad Pin
P. Calvesbert • 56 x 54 x 15
Issued: 1997 • Closed
Market Value: $15

Redemption

2   RW98LI

Behold The King
D. Lawrence • 92 x 70 x 91
Issued: 1998 • Closed
Market Value: $90

3   RW96WH

Big Blue
P. Calvesbert • 154 x 114 x 119
Issued: 1996 • Closed
Market Value: $240

Members Only

Date Purchased	Price Paid	Value
1.		

Redemption

2.		
3.		
4.		

Totals

4   RW97WH

Big Blue
P. Calvesbert • 154 x 114 x 119
Issued: 1997 • Closed
Market Value: $170

1   RW00BB

New!

Byron & Bumbles
M. Baldwin • 76 x 64 x 107
Issued: 2000 • Current
Market Value: $75

2   RW99LB

Byron's Lonely Hearts Club
M. Baldwin • 92 x 76 x 75
Issued: 1999 • Closed
Market Value: N/E

3   RW00MA

New!

Cow Town
D. Lawrence • 89 x 127 x 70
Issued: 2000 • Current
Market Value: $75

4   RW98MU

The Mushroom
M. Perry • 83 x 87 x 106
Issued: 1998 • Closed
Market Value: $85

5   RW99PE

Pell Mell
D. Lawrence • 88 x 90 x 112
Issued: 1999 • Closed
Market Value: N/E

Redemption

	Date Purchased	Price Paid	Value
1.			
2.			
3.			
4.			
5.			

Totals

1 — RW97SU

The Sunflower
M. Perry • 59 x 70 x 122
Issued: 1997 • Closed
Market Value: $130

Special Membership Pieces

2 — RW96

The Big Day
P. Calvesbert • 58 x 35 x 80
Issued: 1996 • Closed
Market Value: $125

3 — RWCTCO

Cotton Anniversary
P. Calvesbert • 60 x 47 x 70
Issued: 1998 • Current
Market Value: $20

Redemption

Date Purchased	Price Paid	Value
1.		

Special Pieces

2.		
3.		
4.		

Totals

4 — RW98TU

Friends of the Royal Watch
D. Lawrence • 36 x 30 x 49
Issued: 1998 • Closed
Market Value: $275

132

Value Guide — Harmony Kingdom®

1   **RWCTLE**

Leather Anniversary
P. Calvesbert • 68 x 45 x 83
Issued: 1999 • Current
Market Value: $20

2   **RWMO**

The Mouse That Roared
P. Calvesbert • 44 x 57 x 89
Issued: 1999 • Closed
Market Value: N/E

3   **RW97PA**

Paper Anniversary
P. Calvesbert • 58 x 60 x 79
Issued: 1997 • Closed
Market Value: $80

4   **RWCTSI**

New!

Silk Anniversary
P. Calvesbert • 51 x 51 x 70
Issued: 2000 • Current
Market Value: $20

5   **RW99DL**

Solemate
D. Lawrence • 58 x 60 x 79
Issued: 1999 • Closed
Market Value: N/E

Special Pieces

	Date Purchased	Price Paid	Value
1.			
2.			
3.			
4.			
5.			
Totals			

133

Picturesque™

Picturesque™

In 1999, Harmony Kingdom took yet another path within the collectible scene and introduced *Picturesque*, intricately crafted tiles. While each tile tells its own story, it can be combined with one or many to form a bigger picture. In addition, The Harmony Ball Company offers boxes on which a tile can be placed, as well as picture frames to house one or all of the tiles.

Byron's Secret Garden

1   PXGB1

Bell Tower
A. Richmond
Issued: 1999 • Current
Market Value: $25

2   PXGB3

Bumble's Bridge
A. Richmond
Issued: 1999 • Current
Market Value: $25

Byron's Secret Garden

	Price Paid	Value
1.		
2.		
3.		
4.		
5.		
6.		
Totals		

3   PXGA4

Byron's Bower
A. Richmond
Issued: 1999 • Current
Market Value: $25

4   PXGD4

Cata's Pillow
A. Richmond
Issued: 1999 • Current
Market Value: $25

5   PXGC2

Fountain Blue
A. Richmond
Issued: 1999 • Current
Market Value: $25

6   PXGE3

A Frog's Life
A. Richmond
Issued: 1999 • Current
Market Value: $25

1   PXGA3

Garter Of Eden
A. Richmond
Issued: 1999 • Current
Market Value: $25

2   PXGD2

Gourmet Gazebo
A. Richmond
Issued: 1999 • Current
Market Value: $25

3   PXGC4

Honey Brew
A. Richmond
Issued: 1999 • Current
Market Value: $25

4   PXGB4

The Long Sleep
A. Richmond
Issued: 1999 • Current
Market Value: $25

5   PXGD3

Love's Labours
A. Richmond
Issued: 1999 • Current
Market Value: $25

6   PXGC1

Martin's Minstrels
A. Richmond
Issued: 1999 • Current
Market Value: $25

7   PXGE4

Mayfly Madame
A. Richmond
Issued: 1999 • Current
Market Value: $25

8   PXGA2

Mum's Reading Room
A. Richmond
Issued: 1999 • Current
Market Value: $25

9   PXGD1

Slow Downs
A. Richmond
Issued: 1999 • Current
Market Value: $25

10   PXGA1

Sun Worshipper
A. Richmond
Issued: 1999 • Current
Market Value: $25

Byron's Secret Garden

	Price Paid	Value
1.		
2.		
3.		
4.		
5.		
6.		
7.		
8.		
9.		
10.		
Totals		

Picturesque™

1 — PXGB2

Swing Time
A. Richmond
Issued: 1999 • Current
Market Value: $25

2 — PXGE1

Two Blind Mice
A. Richmond
Issued: 1999 • Current
Market Value: $25

3 — PXGE2
Webmaster's Woe
A. Richmond
Issued: 1999 • Current
Market Value: $25

4 — PXGC3

Zen Garden
A. Richmond
Issued: 1999 • Current
Market Value: $25

Noah's Park

5 — PXNA3

Beaky's Beach
A. Richmond
Issued: 1999 • Current
Market Value: $25

6 — PXNB3

Bungees In The Mist
A. Richmond
Issued: 1999 • Current
Market Value: $25

7 — PXND2

Cliff Hangers
A. Richmond
Issued: 1999 • Current
Market Value: $25

8 — PXNE2

Dolphin Downs
A. Richmond
Issued: 1999 • Current
Market Value: $25

9 — PXND4

Flamingo East
A. Richmond
Issued: 1999 • Current
Market Value: $25

Byron's Secret Garden

	Price Paid	Value
1.		
2.		
3.		
4.		

Noah's Park

5.		
6.		
7.		
8.		
9.		
Totals		

Value Guide—Harmony Kingdom®

1   PXND3

Flume Lagoon
A. Richmond
Issued: 1999 • Current
Market Value: $25

2   PXNE3

Glacier Falls
A. Richmond
Issued: 1999 • Current
Market Value: $25

3   PXNC3

Heart Of Darkness
A. Richmond
Issued: 1999 • Current
Market Value: $25

4   PXNB2

Krakatoa Lounge
A. Richmond
Issued: 1999 • Current
Market Value: $25

5   PXNC1

The Lost Ark
P. Calvesbert
Issued: 1999 • Current
Market Value: $25

6   PXNC2

Mark of the Beast
A. Richmond
Issued: 1999 • Current
Market Value: $25

7   PXNE4

Nessie's Nook
A. Richmond
Issued: 1999 • Current
Market Value: $25

8   PXNB4

Pelican Bay
A. Richmond
Issued: 1999 • Current
Market Value: $25

9   PXNA4

Point Siren Song
A. Richmond
Issued: 1999 • Current
Market Value: $25

10   PXNA1

Sky Master
A. Richmond
Issued: 1999 • Current
Market Value: $25

Noah's Park

	Price Paid	Value
1.		
2.		
3.		
4.		
5.		
6.		
7.		
8.		
9.		
10.		
Totals		

Value Guide—Harmony Kingdom®

1 PXNB1

Sun Catcher
A. Richmond
Issued: 1999 • Current
Market Value: $25

2 PXNE1

Thunder Dome
A. Richmond
Issued: 1999 • Current
Market Value: $25

3 PXNC4

Tilt-A-Whirl
A. Richmond
Issued: 1999 • Current
Market Value: $25

4 PXNA2

Whale Watch
A. Richmond
Issued: 1999 • Current
Market Value: $25

5 PXND1

Whirligig Rainbow
A. Richmond
Issued: 1999 • Current
Market Value: $25

Wimberley Tales

6 New! PXWD1

The Artist
M. Ricketts
Issued: 2000 • Current
Market Value: $35

7 New! PXWD4

The Baker
M. Ricketts
Issued: 2000 • Current
Market Value: $35

8 New! PXWD3

The Birthday
M. Ricketts
Issued: 2000 • Current
Market Value: $35

9 New! PXWA1

The Builder
M. Ricketts
Issued: 2000 • Current
Market Value: $35

Noah's Park

	Price Paid	Value
1.		
2.		
3.		
4.		
5.		

Wimberley Tales

6.		
7.		
8.		
9.		

Totals

Value Guide—Harmony Kingdom®

1 New! PXWD5

The Butcher
M. Ricketts
Issued: 2000 • Current
Market Value: $35

2 New! PXWA3

The Chef
M. Ricketts
Issued: 2000 • Current
Market Value: $35

3 New! PXWC1

The Chimney
M. Ricketts
Issued: 2000 • Current
Market Value: $25

4 New! PXWB1

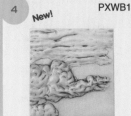

The Clouds
M. Ricketts
Issued: 2000 • Current
Market Value: $25

5 New! PXWA5

The Dentist
M. Ricketts
Issued: 2000 • Current
Market Value: $35

6 New! PXWA4

The Doctor
M. Ricketts
Issued: 2000 • Current
Market Value: $35

7 New! PXWB4

The Fireman
M. Ricketts
Issued: 2000 • Current
Market Value: $25

8 New! PXWB5

The Harlot
M. Ricketts
Issued: 2000 • Current
Market Value: $35

9 New! PXWD2

The Lawyer
M. Ricketts
Issued: 2000 • Current
Market Value: $35

10 New! PXWC3

The Lovers
M. Ricketts
Issued: 2000 • Current
Market Value: $35

Wimberley Tales

	Price Paid	Value
1.		
2.		
3.		
4.		
5.		
6.		
7.		
8.		
9.		
10.		
Totals		

Picturesque™

1 New! **PXWC5**

The Masquerade
M. Ricketts
Issued: 2000 • Current
Market Value: $35

2 New! **PXWC2**

The Rooftop
M. Ricketts
Issued: 2000 • Current
Market Value: $35

3 New! **PXWA2**

The Scientist
M. Ricketts
Issued: 2000 • Current
Market Value: $35

4 New! **PXWB3**

The Sea
M. Ricketts
Issued: 2000 • Current
Market Value: $25

5 New! **PXWB2**

The Sun
M. Ricketts
Issued: 2000 • Current
Market Value: $25

6 New! **PXWC4**

The Teacher
M. Ricketts
Issued: 2000 • Current
Market Value: $35

Wimberley Tales

	Price Paid	Value
1.		
2.		
3.		
4.		
5.		
6.		

Limited Edition Tiles

7.		
8.		
9.		

Totals

Limited Edition Tiles

7 **PXXMASCA**

Purrfect Tidings
A. Richmond
Issued: 1999 • Current
Market Value: $55

8 **PXXMASHO**

Ruffians' Feast
A. Richmond
Issued: 1999 • Current
Market Value: $55

9 **PXPC1**

Storm Brewing
P. Calvesbert
Issued: 1999 • Current
Market Value: $55

Value Guide—Harmony Kingdom®

Tile Boxes

1 PXGBOX

Byron's Hideaway
A. Richmond
Issued: 1999 • Current
Market Value: $55

2 PXNBOX

Noah's Hideaway
A. Richmond
Issued: 1999 • Current
Market Value: $55
Variation Value: $75 (event box)

Frames

3 N/A

Picturesque Box Frame
N/A
Issued: 1999 • Current
Market Value: $35

4 N/A

*Picturesque Bryon's
Secret Garden 20
Tile Frame*
N/A
Issued: 1999 • Current
Market Value: $50

5 N/A

*Picturesque Noah's Park
20 Tile Frame*
N/A
Issued: 1999 • Current
Market Value: $50

6 N/A

*Picturesque Single Tile
Frame*
N/A
Issued: 1999 • Current
Market Value: $6

Tile Boxes

	Price Paid	Value
1.		
2.		

Frames

	Price Paid	Value
3.		
4.		
5.		
6.		

Totals

Future Releases

Use this page to record future Harmony Kingdom® releases.

Harmony Kingdom	Code	Artist	Size	Issue Year	Status	Price Paid	Market Value

Page Total:	Price Paid	Total Value

Future Releases

Use this page to record future Harmony Kingdom® releases.

Harmony Kingdom	Code	Artist	Size	Issue Year	Status	Price Paid	Market Value

	Price Paid	Total Value
Page Total:		

Total Value Of My Collection

Add the "Page Totals" together to find the "Grand Total."

Harmony Kingdom			Harmony Kingdom		
Page Number	Price Paid	Market Value	Page Number	Price Paid	Market Value
Page 49			Page 71		
Page 50			Page 72		
Page 51			Page 73		
Page 52			Page 74		
Page 53			Page 75		
Page 54			Page 76		
Page 55			Page 77		
Page 56			Page 78		
Page 57			Page 79		
Page 58			Page 80		
Page 59			Page 81		
Page 60			Page 82		
Page 61			Page 83		
Page 62			Page 84		
Page 63			Page 85		
Page 64			Page 86		
Page 65			Page 87		
Page 66			Page 88		
Page 67			Page 89		
Page 68			Page 90		
Page 69			Page 91		
Page 70			Page 92		
			Page 93		
Subtotal:			Subtotal:		

Page Total:	Price Paid	Value

Total Value Of My Collection

Harmony Kingdom			Harmony Kingdom		
Page Number	Price Paid	Market Value	Page Number	Price Paid	Market Value
Page 94			Page 118		
Page 95			Page 119		
Page 96			Page 120		
Page 97			Page 121		
Page 98			Page 122		
Page 99			Page 123		
Page 100			Page 124		
Page 101			Page 125		
Page 102			Page 126		
Page 103			Page 127		
Page 104			Page 128		
Page 105			Page 129		
Page 106			Page 130		
Page 107			Page 131		
Page 108			Page 132		
Page 109			Page 133		
Page 110			Page 134		
Page 111			Page 135		
Page 112			Page 136		
Page 113			Page 137		
Page 114			Page 138		
Page 115			Page 139		
Page 116			Page 140		
Page 117			Page 141		
Page 118			Page 142		
			Page 143		
Subtotal:			Subtotal:		

Page Total:	Price Paid	Value

GRAND TOTAL:	Price Paid	Value

Harmony Kingdom® Live

The moment collectors arrive it all takes their breath away – the fragrant flowers, the trickle of a waterfall, the sounds of baby goats. Then, ever so slowly, the crowds gather around, the noise rushes in and collectors soon find themselves, not in the middle of a serene country field as it seems, but in the center of Harmony Kingdom's booth at one of various collectible expositions. This booth and the activities surrounding it certainly become the talk of the show.

Booth director, Chris Clements, has much to be proud of and this has not gone without official acknowledgement. At the 1999 Long Beach Convention, the booth received the honor of Best Booth. At the Rosemont show, it was honored once again as runner-up in that category.

The 1999 Rosemont show was quite an adventure. Before reaching the Harmony Kingdom booth, collectors were clued in to what they were in for. Flags flew high above the booth, signifying each of Harmony Kingdom's Independent Clubs. A procession of bagpipes that at first were distant, ever so slowly came right down the aisles, as if telling collectors to follow behind and they'd be led to a magical world. Upon arrival, they found a small, fenced-in area which held Hamlet the pig, as children of all ages gasped at the huge animal nestled in ankle-deep hay. Hamlet was accompanied by two baby goats that could have easily stolen the show with their kid-like behavior. And although it was 100 degrees outside, the abundance of flowers in Harmony Kingdom's booth made it feel more like a breezy

day in Spring. Ivy crept along the towering rock walls, as hydrangea and other fragrant blooms sprouted about. It was the perfect place for Lord Byron to pay a visit, which in fact, he did. The giant lady-

bug surprised many collectors with his appearance, just as he does in his travels through Harmony Garden.

When it was time to make themselves known to those who had not yet made it to the booth, the bagpipers once again struck a harmonious chord and off they went. Representatives from The Harmony Ball Company, dressed in Renaissance garb, descended from their thrones and sauntered through the aisles, as if on their way to a

royal event. Members of the Independent Clubs followed, raising high their individual banners, a display of how proud they were to be a part of the spectacular show. Curious onlookers watched in amazement as Harmony Kingdom took center stage.

At any show, although the scenery and activity are always brilliant, the main focus of Harmony Kingdom's booth is, to no surprise, the artists and their fabulous creations. At each show, the artists take on a sort of celebrity status and put themselves at the disposal of hundreds of collectors who stand in lines that at times wrap around the booth. And these artists recognize the importance of their fans and relish in this opportunity to speak to each one individually, as well as to sign their pieces.

While the scenery and artist signings are very responsible for the attraction scene, the booth also offers much more. Knowledgeable representatives from The Harmony Ball

Company are always on hand to walk the retailer and collector through the line, answer any questions and reveal information. The co-owners and founders, Noel Wiggins and Lisa Yashon, who have

achieved celebrity status in their own right, are also always present and enthusiastic to speak with the plethora of Harmony Kingdom fans.

This enthusiasm has paid off. The collectors who flock to the booth are a loyal bunch and a sight of their own. And they come prepared: some with suitcases packed with pieces, giving the unsuspecting convention goer the idea that these bag toters have just come from the airport – never imagining the cases are filled to the brim with pieces to be signed.

And as quickly as the festivities began, they end. The flowers are uprooted and the animals taken back to the farm. The artists head back to the drawing board, the Independent Clubs' banners are packed away and the magical booth becomes just another part of the convention hall. It's like waking up from a wonderful dream. But that's okay – collectors know there's always next year and with each

passing year, the journey to this fairy tale world becomes even more of an adventure.

Secondary Market Overview

In the world of collecting, the secondary market is very important. It's the place to turn when searching for a piece that can't be found in retail stores. It's been known to happen: ever since you began collecting Harmony Kingdom, you've wanted a copy of "Neighborhood Watch" – but you can't seem to find it anywhere! Don't despair. Whether the piece you're looking for is five years old, exclusive, or retired, you have a good chance of finding it on the secondary market. So where can you find the secondary market? In the past, collectors have relied on newspaper classifieds, flea markets and even word of mouth. But in recent years, the most prevalent source of information has become the Internet.

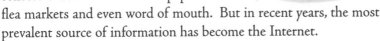

Within the past few years, computers have become a household staple, making the Internet accessible to almost everyone. Going on-line has become a way of life; as a result, shopping the secondary market has become quite convenient. The Internet offers you the freedom to search all sorts of options without ever leaving the comfort of your own home.

One of the most exciting reasons to use the Internet is the chance to stumble upon pieces that have long since left the shelves of retail stores. However, some pieces are occasionally reissued, so keep a sharp eye! Many Harmony Kingdom boxes have been retired, or were produced in very small quantities. Members of *The Elusive Few* are very hard to find, simply because they were produced in very small numbers, and very few of them made it to the United States. Other boxes are hard to find because they are limited editions, like the *Holiday* pieces. These pieces are only available for a certain time or merit a specified amount of carvings before their molds are broken. Royal Watch Collector's Club pieces are also highly sought after as they are available for only one year and only to club members. Limited editions, exclusives, special event pieces and pieces signed by the artist can become an exciting find. But if you are interested in pieces like this, don't expect to find them with the other Harmony Kingdom pieces at your local collectibles shop. But rest assured, all of these pieces are out there . . . you just have to know where to look.

There are hundreds, if not thousands, of websites about Harmony Kingdom and other collectibles. You can find information ranging from pictures of an individual's collection to up-to-date price lists and pictures for every piece. Sometimes these lists come from secondary market dealers, who also offer information about contacting them if you're interested in their inventory.

Not only is there plenty of information on personal websites, but also in chat rooms and on bulletin boards. These locations offer the ability to communicate one-on-one, or even as a group, with collectors who have the same interests. Who knows – you may find someone trying to sell the very piece for which you've been looking.

One of the most popular ways to locate that hard-to-find piece is on one of the countless on-line auction sites. The more popular auctions have numerous listing for all kinds of collectibles. For example, at the time of this printing, one site had more than 1,700 listings for Harmony Kingdom. All you have to do is type in a search for "Harmony Kingdom," or even the individual box's name, and you're suddenly exposed to an entire world of pieces for sale. Don't be surprised if you suddenly find multiple listings for that one special box you thought you'd never find.

These sites also offer the chance to do some comparison shopping. Seeing what others are paying for their pieces can be helpful in determining the amount you're willing to bid on the piece you want to buy.

With that in mind, remember to be very thorough in researching the piece's condition. Often times, a picture will accompany a piece's description. In order to protect yourself, make sure the photo is of the actual piece you will be receiving, not just an example of what it looks like. Don't hesitate to e-mail the seller and ask. On most sites, placing a bid is equivalent to signing a contract, and if you're the highest bidder, it becomes your responsibility to buy.

It's also wise to make sure that the seller is reputable. Check to see if the auction site has a feedback rating section where sellers are rated by previous buyers. If the seller is a dealer, you might be able to obtain additional information through The Better Business Bureau (*www.BBBonline.org*). Remember that this should be a stress-free hobby, and doing a little homework in the beginning can save a lot of heartache, and money, in the end.

There are also other more personal means to finding your pieces. Swap & sells are one of the most popular. These events usually bring out collectors from all over the state, region or even country. Usually there are rows of tables stocked full of merchandise. Flea markets also the offer this type of atmosphere. The classifieds section of the newspaper offers another route, usually on a local level.

Most retailers do not take part in the secondary market; however, they can act as a liaison between collectors. Some retailers provide lists of collectors looking to buy, sell or trade pieces, as well as information pertaining to swap & sells around the area.

So how much should you pay for a piece? As with all collectibles, there are things that make two of the same design differ in value. One is the overall condition. If a piece is said to be in perfect condition, it is considered "mint." This means there is nothing faulty with the piece, and the box (also in perfect condition) should be included, as well as any literature that came with the piece. This holds especially true if the piece is an exclusive or limited edition. If a piece is anything but "mint," ask the seller to explain the defect. As a general rule, prices listed in value guides such as the Collector's Value Guide™ are for pieces that are in "mint" or "near-mint" condition. Many of the earlier pieces were often sold without their original boxes, thus they are considered "near-mint." Anything in less than "mint" condition will have a lower value, and in turn, the price you pay should be lower.

Another factor that can decide the value of an individual piece is a variation. In the world of Harmony Kingdom, a lot of these variations are planned, and are referred to as "versions." The company usually produces a set number called "Version 1." This first version is usually the one that demands the higher value as it is limited in quality and the older of the pieces.

However, due to the hand-crafted process in which the pieces are made, unintentional variations in color and design often occur (*see Variation* section on page 153 for a more detailed explanation). For example, collectors have found at least three color variations so far in "Trumpeters' Ball." Yet, it is impossible to predict which of these types of variations will increase the monetary value of the piece. However, they almost all increase collector interest.

One of the most important things to keep in mind when shopping on the secondary market is why you are there. Don't let yourself be talked into something you don't want or weren't looking for in the first place. Collecting Harmony Kingdom boxes, as well as any collectible, is a fun hobby, and the hunt for a piece should make it even more exciting – not stressful or expensive.

Change is a common occurrence in the world of collectibles. It comes in all shapes, sizes and colors, and happens for a variety of reasons. For many Harmony Kingdom pieces, changes are created intentionally, as the artist will sculpt more than one "version." The change may be as small as one part of the piece being painted a different color, to something as big as a mold change. But whatever the reason, it gives the collectors a chance at finding more than one version of their favorite piece.

There are also unintentional changes which are considered variations, and most occur when the first production run of a piece is not compatible for some reason and the mold must be changed. The exciting part of Harmony Kingdom's variations is that they exist in almost every piece, whether intentional or not. Please note that this section is merely a sample of the differences in the Harmony Kingdom boxes, and includes pieces which may or may not hold significant value on the secondary market.

Alegnon: This piece was first released in 1998. The original version contains Peter Calvesbert bathing in the company of his rubber ducky. Under the lid is a reference to an old acquaintance, wondering where she has gone. He also added his e-mail address so this lost "ZOE BAIN" could contact him. The second version of "Algenon" contains balls of yarn and a pair of knitting needles on the inside. and the e-mail address has been omitted.

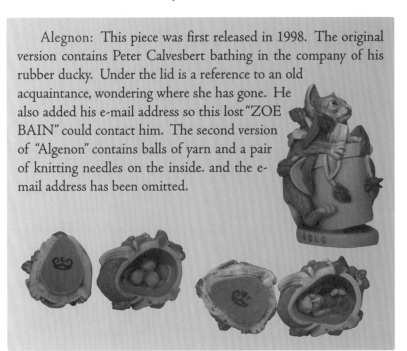

Bamboozled: Being the animal enthusiast that he is, Peter Calvesbert carved this piece to represent the deteriorating panda population and the bamboo forests in which they live. The interior of the first version has a tombstone on which "1000 to Save" is inscribed. On the second version, the number has increased to 1006, representing 6 more pandas that had been located. Apparently, there were also production difficulties with the first version's mold, so it was re-shaped in order to make the space between the panda's arms wider and the tinting of the bamboo shoots changed as well.

Big Blue: In the case of "Big Blue," the variation is as easy as a club piece being offered two years in a row with different inscriptions. In 1996, the piece was available as a redemption piece to charter members of the Royal Watch Collector's Club. On the base it reads, "Royal Watch Charter 1996." The same piece was offered the next year, but only reads "Royal Watch 1997," although some mistakenly say "Royal Watch Charter 1997."

The Big Day: It's no secret that brides try on many different wedding dresses before finding the one they really love. But in this piece, it's Peter who can't seem to decide how to dress for "The Big Day." The groom went through an extensive pallette of jacket colors, including white, brown, grey, and black, and even switched between black shoes and white shoes before finally walking down the aisle.

Brean Sands: Very few pieces of "Brean Sands" actually came away from production as intended, which was supposed to be with an empty interior. The first 100 or so have a hand inside. The interior was later changed to house a treasure chest. This same version has been colored white, a rare find in the United States.

Catch A Lot: The whale seems to have almost caught Jonah (Peter?) in the first version of "Catch A Lot." Inside, the surprised boater tries furiously to make his way through the hull of the boat, as to escape the man-eating whale. In Version 2, the opposite has happened, and the boat is full of crazed sight-seers chasing the whale in hopes of getting a glimpse. A third version depicts a rain slicker-adorning dog.

Croc Pot: This piece quickly became two versions due to a production change that had to be made in order to avoid possible trademark infringement. Included in the interior of the first version is an empty hamburger box with a familiar golden "M." The letter was later changed, and the second version now has "HK" on the box.

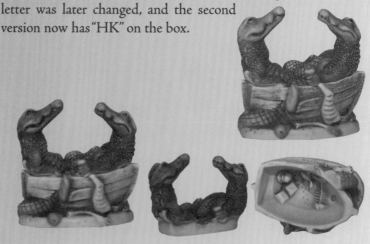

Family Reunion: When a family comes together, there is always something different this time around from the last time. This piece holds some of that truth. As a healthy diet involves variety, this piece appeared with orange, red and yellow berries.

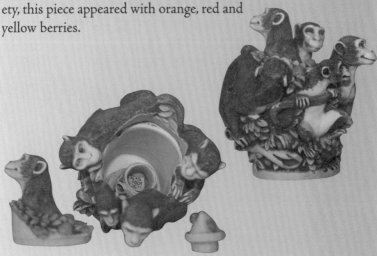

Friends In High Places: The mouse that is hidden ever-so-subtly in most of Peter Calvesbert's carvings is on the run in this piece. In the initial "Friends In High Places," the mouse is hiding beneath the chin of one of the giraffes. It was soon realized that, even though he's trying to hide, he was doing an all-to-well job of it. So, the mold was changed, and on the altered pieces, the mouse is happily resting in between one of the lion cub's paws.

Killing Time: Not only is this piece special because of its limited quality, but also because the frequent coloration changes that occurred in the short amount of time it was available. When "Killing Time" was first released, the sand on the box was painted black. Due to production difficulties, the color of the sand was soon changed to pale yellow. But the new change was not well-received, so the original color of black was reinstated.

Nic Nac Paddy Whack: Besides the name being spelled several different ways, this piece was, at one time, very bright. One of the dogs in the earlier releases was a rich red color. Now, the dog has been toned down a bit. Also, the inside of the box houses a boot, whether it's the right one or the left one is a surprise to collectors.

Petty Teddies: Perhaps it's the original name of "Perished Teddies" that gained this teddy bear-hacking piece its popularity. Inside is a replica of a decapitated doll-like figurine lying next to a hatchet. The Infinity Version's interior shows Peter and several dismembered teddies, obvious losers in the battle with the two dogs on the outside of the box. Soon after its release in January 1999, the piece's name was changed to "Petty Teddies."

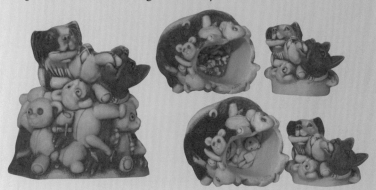

Pillow Talk: When this gorgeous *Romance Annual* was first released, the two swans had red beaks. The two compartments contained a white rose in remembrance of Princess Diana, and the other contained a blue pillow which could be removed to uncover a red heart. On the second version, the beaks are painted yellow, but the pillow remains blue. Finally on the third version, the interior pillow is green and the beaks remain yellow.

Pondering: Although this is one of the extremely early pieces, "Pondering" has two different interiors: a cracked egg and no egg. Although there is only a slight difference in monetary value, collectors still treasure both versions because of how long the piece has been around.

Rumble Seat: Apparently this is a hot seat to have! When this group of cats was first released, the chair which they are gathered around was brown. Sixty-six boxes later, the chair was painted green. Soon after, the chair was painted yellow.

Swap 'n Sell: This piece became quite popular during the 1999 International Collectible Expositions in both Long Beach and Rosemont. The reason? Only 2,500 were available to collectors at each show. Also some offered collectors a small glimpse into Peter Calvesbert's private life, as his private parts are covered with a pair of Groucho Marx glasses. However, most of the interiors sport the redesign which features a fig leaf instead of the shades.

Trumpeters' Ball: These pachyderms have been through a variety of changes since they were released in June 1996. When first introduced, the group of elephants in "Trumpeters' Ball" were painted yellow and grey. Next came less than 500 pieces which were colorless. In the remainder of the pieces, two elephants are grey. Oddly, there was an extra trunk on the piece, but it was removed from the production mold soon after the piece's release.

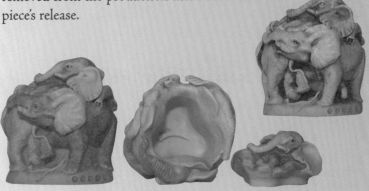

Unbearables: Originally, this limited edition box figurine was released with nothing on the inside. But after almost 800 empty boxes, a miniature replica of the title piece was added to the interior. There was a total of only 2,500 boxes released, so the empty one is truly a hard one to find.

Wishful Thinking: On the inside of the first version, an inscription reads, "VVEJGA," meaning Venus, Earth, Jupiter Gravity Assisted. Also on this version is the estimated date the Cassini Space Probe will reach Saturn. The interior of Version 2 contains a pair of running shoes and a speed limit sign. An inscription reads "C. Huygens 1655" in reference to the man who discovered Titan, one of Saturn's many moons. Various products also show up underneath the table on the outside of these versions, including a half screw and a cigarette lighter.

Insuring Your Collection

W hen insuring your collection, there are three major points
to consider:

1. Know Your Coverage: Collectibles are
typically included in homeowner's or renter's
insurance policies. Ask your agent if your
policy covers fire, theft, floods, hurricanes,
earthquakes and damage or breakage from routine
handling. Also, ask if your policy covers claims at "current replacement value" – the amount it would cost to replace items
if they were damaged, lost or stolen. This is extremely important
since the secondary market value of some pieces may well exceed
their original retail price.

2. Document Your Collection: In the
event of a loss, you will need a record of the
contents and value of your collection.
Ask your insurance agent what information is acceptable. Keep receipts and an
inventory of your collection in a different
location, such as a safe deposit box. Include the purchase date, price
paid, size, issue year, edition limit/number, special markings and secondary market value for each piece. Photographs and video footage
with close-up views of each piece, including tags, boxes and signa-
tures, are good back-ups.

3. Weigh The Risk: To determine the coverage you need, calculate how much it would cost to replace your collection and compare it to the total amount your current policy would pay. To insure
your collection for a specific dollar amount, ask your agent about
adding a Personal Articles Floater or a Fine
Arts Floater or "rider" to your policy, or
insuring your collection under a sepa-
rate policy. As with all insurance, you
must weigh the risk of loss against the
cost of additional coverage.

Building The Kingdom

The figurines and boxes of Harmony Kingdom are not mass-produced pieces, churned out in large numbers by a machine. Each one is an original artist's design, created by an imaginative mind, carved by skilled hands and finished by talented

people. There's a lot of work that goes into creating a Harmony Kingdom piece – work that guarantees a beautifully crafted piece that will be cherished for years.

After designing the piece, the artist will then begin to carve an original. A mixture of clay and plasticine is used, and after enduring all the artist's finishing touches, the original is ready for a mold to be made from it. That original carving is destroyed soon after.

An original carving will yield one original mold, and that original mold leads to twelve master molds. This is where the artists often like to exercise their creative sides by creating variations within their pieces. These changes are always made to the master molds, never the original. More molds are made from those twelve masters, cast in silicon rubber.

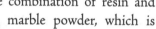

Harmony Kingdom's pieces are made from a unique combination of resin and marble powder, which is

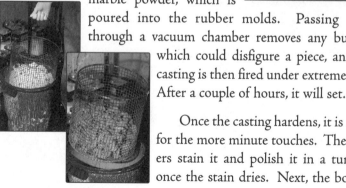

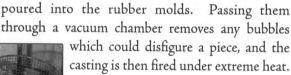

poured into the rubber molds. Passing them through a vacuum chamber removes any bubbles which could disfigure a piece, and the casting is then fired under extreme heat. After a couple of hours, it will set.

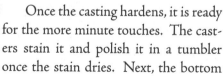

Once the casting hardens, it is ready for the more minute touches. The casters stain it and polish it in a tumbler once the stain dries. Next, the bottom of the piece is sanded smooth. At this point, it has to go through an inspection. If the smooth base is unpolished, or if there is some kind of imperfection, it won't receive the Harmony Kingdom stamp. The artists who carve these pieces wouldn't dream of putting their name or stamp on a piece that was less than perfect!

Then it's time to give the piece a little color. It goes to the Painting Department at the factory, or sometimes to people working out of their homes. The piece is meticulously hand-painted, and must pass another inspection before being packaged and shipped to retailers. Its next stop may well be your mantel!

This process for creating Harmony Kingdom's unique figures has changed little over the years – but the demand for them has induced the company to increase production. Originally, the work was done at Griffin Mill, a facility in the English countryside. But when the work proved to be too much for a small location to handle, production was moved to Wimberley Mills, its current home in the

South Cotswolds. Even that wasn't enough. In 1997, the demand for Martin Perry's *Lord Byron's Harmony Garden* line was so great that the line's production was moved to China.

But no matter where they are made, Harmony Kingdom's attention to artistic detail and superior quality work has never disappointed collectors – and it looks like it's going to stay that way.

Carving Dates

The Harmony Ball Company documents the year during which the artists' creation becomes finalized. This date is referred to as the Carving Date. Below is a list of the Harmony Kingdom pieces and their Carving Dates. Please note that this year is usually different from the year in which the piece is released.

1990

Drake's Fancy
Keeping Current
Pondering
Quiet Waters
Ram
Step Aside
Who'd A Thought

1991

Awaiting A Kiss
Horn A' Plenty
Journey Home
Pen Pals
Rooster, Large
Straight From The Hip
Sunnyside Up
Tea For Two

1992

40 Winks
On A Roll
Princely Thoughts
Side Steppin'

1993

All Ears
All Tied Up
At Arm's Length
Baby On Board
Back Scratch
Day Dreamer
Hammin' It Up
It's A Fine Day
Jonah's Hideaway
Of The Same Stripe
One Step Ahead
Panda
Pride And Joy
Reminiscence
Rooster (Cockerel)
School's Out
Shark
Sheep (Shaggy) Dog
Shell Game
Standing Guard
Swamp Song
Top Banana
Trunk Show

1994

All Angles Covered
Antarctic Antics
Dog Days
Family Tree
Group Therapy
Hold That Line
Horse Play
Inside Joke
Let's Do Lunch
Life's A Picnic
Love Seat
Mad Dogs And
    Englishmen
Neighborhood Watch
Play School
Purrfect Friends
Sunday Swim
Teacher's Pet
Tongue And Cheek
Too Much Of A Good
    Thing
Unbearables
Unexpected Arrival
Untouchable
Wise Guys

1995

1996 Frog Pendant
1998 Edison Lovebird
    Pin
Angel Baroque
At The Hop
The Audience
Ball Brothers
Baroness Trotter
Beak To Beak
Beppo And Barney
    The Clowns
Big Blue
The Big Day
Chatelaine
Courtiers At Rest

Damnable Plot
Den Mothers
Ed's Safari
Fur Ball
Garden Prince
Great Escapo
Henry The Human
    Cannonball
Holding Court
Il Bendi
Jersey Belles
Lionel Loveless
Magician's Top Hat
Major's Mousers
Mud Bath
Nick Of Time
Noah's Lark
Olde Time Carousel
Open Mike
Paradise Found
Paradise Lost
Pavareata
Primordial Soup
Puddle Huddle
Purrfect Fit
Rather Large Friends
Rather Large Hop
Rather Large Huddle
Rather Large Safari
Road Dogs
Royal Flotilla
Shoebill
Sweet Serenade
Teapot Angel I
Teapot Angel II
Unbridled & Groomed
Vlad The Impaler
Winston The Lion Tamer
Yeoman Of The Guard

1996

1997 Rose Pendant
1998 Angel Pendant
The Arch
Bewear The Hare
Boarding School
Bon Chance

Bon Enfant
Bozini The Clown
Brean Sands
Cat's Cradle
Cat's Cradle Too
Celeste
Changing Of The
    Guard
Chrysanthemum
Chucky Pig
Circus Ring
Clever Constantine
Close Shave
Count Belfry
Cranberry
Daisy
Down Under
Dragon Breath
Duc De Lyon
Earl Of Oswald
Fleur-de-lis
Friends In High
    Places
Gentil Homme
Harmony Bull
Have A Heart
Hog Heaven
Hyacinth
Hydrangea
Ingenue
Joie De Vivre
Killing Time
Kitty's Kipper
Ladies In Waiting
Liberty And Justice
Lord Busby
Madeline Of The
    High Wire
Major Parker
Marquis De Blanc
Marsh Marigold
Morning Glory
The Mouse
    That Roared
Mr. Sediment's
    Superior Victuals
Mutton Chops

Nic Nac Paddy Whack
Oktobearfest
Paper Anniversary
Peace Lily
Peace Offering
Photo Finish
Pink Paradise
Pumpkinfest
Queen's Counsel
Rhododendron
The Ringmaster
Rumble Seat
Sleepy Hollow
Snow Drop
Solemate
Suave St. John
Sweet As A
  Summer's Kiss
Thin Ice
Tin Cat
Toad Pin
Trumpeters' Ball
Whale Of A Time

1997

1997 Puffin Pin
Algenon
Antipasto
April's Fool Pewter Pen
Aria Amorosa
Baby Boomer
Bamboozled
Begonia
Behold The King
Cactus
Cat Pin
Croc Pot
Double Pink Rose
Double Red Rose
Double Violet Rose
Double Yellow Rose
Driver's Seat
Fab Five
Family Reunion
Faux Paw
Forget Me Not
Friends of the Royal
  Watch
Gardenia
In Fine Feather
Iris
Ivory Tower
Murphy's Last Stand
The Mushroom
Original Kin
Peony
Pieces Of Eight

Pillow Talk
Play Ball
Pooh And Friends
Rocky's Raiders
Rose Basket
Rose Bud
Rose Party
Scratching Post
  Pewter Pen
Single Orange Rose
Single Pink Rose
Single Red Rose
Single Violet Rose
Single White Rose
Single Yellow Rose
Snapdragon
Something's Gotta Give
Splashdown
Sterling Rose
Sunflower
The Sunflower
Tabby Totem Pewter
  Pen
Terra Incognita
Tony's Tabbies
Wishful Thinking

1998

1998 Holiday
  Ornament Set
1999 Lord Byron
  Pendant
Alpine Flower
Beneath the Ever
  Changing Seas
Byron's Lonely Hearts
  Club
Camelot
Catch A Lot
Christmas Bouquet
Cotton Anniversary
Crackin' Brew
Dead Ringer
Double Sterling Rose
Easter Bouquet
Ed's Safari II
Foul Play
Gill
Halloween Bouquet
Helen the Owl
Holy Roller
Hops
Hot Pepper
Jewels Of The Wild
Jingle Bell Rock
Joyeaux
La Gardienne

Leather Anniversary
Lion King's Pride Rock
Love Nest
Marigold
Marty the Polar Bear
Ménage Å Trois
Mother's Day Boquet
Murphy Pin
Noel
Orange
Package Tour
Parade of Gifts
Peace Summit
Pell Mell
Pet Parade
Petty Teddies
Pip the Pelican
Pomegranate
Primordial Sloop
Queen of the Jungle
Road Kill
Sin City
Sneak Preview
Snow White
Sunflower II
Swap 'n Sell
Tally Ho!
Tin Cat's Cruise
Tubs Pin
Tulip
When Nature Calls
Y2hk
Zephyr the Monkey

1999

1999 Lord
  Byron Pendant
Albatross
Bon Bon
Byron & Bumbles
Catch As Catch Can
Cat's Meow
Caw Of The Wild
Cherry Blossom
Clair de Lune
Clair's Cat
Cookie's Jar
Cow Town
Creature Comforts
Crooze Cat
Disorderly Eating
Ed's Safari III
Egyptian Rose
Field Day
Fusspot
Gobblefest
The Good Race

Grapes
The Great Escape
Harry
Home Sweet Home
Jump Shot
The Last Laugh
Lemon
Lotus
Lover's Leap
Manatee Wee Beastie
Merry-Go-Round
Moggy Bag
Nell
Ollie
Pacer the Greyhound
Pastille
Pecking Order
Pinocchio's Great
  Adventure
Poppy
Pot Sticker
QVC Pin
Retired Racers
Silk Anniversary
Snowdonia Fields
Special Delivery
Spring Bouquet
Squee
Sterling Silver
  Baroness Trotter
Sterling Silver
  Garden Prince
Sterling Silver Lord
  Byron
Summer Bouquet
Tarka
Tender Is The Night
Trunk Call
Turdus Felidae
Waddles
Yt42hk

Glossary

Carving Date – the date that the artist's carving becomes finalized.

Collectible – anything and everything that is "able to be collected." Figurines, dolls, even *beer mugs* can be considered a "collectible," but it is generally recognized that a true collectible should be something that increases in value over time.

Current – any piece which has not yet been retired and is still available in stores.

Event Piece – a figurine or box which was carved for a specific happening, such as a collectibles convention, a trade show or even a cruise.

Exclusive Piece – an item which is only available through certain retail outlets or to members of the Royal Watch™ Collector's Club.

Hallmark – a special engraving or stamp on an individual piece which gives information about that piece.

International Collectible Exposition – a national collectible show held annually in June in the Midwest and in April alternating between the East and West coasts.

Introduction Date – the date a particular piece is offered to official dealers.

Limited Edition (LE) – a piece scheduled for a predetermined production quantity or time period.

Primary Market – the conventional collectibles purchasing process in which collectors buy directly from dealers at retail price.

Retired – a piece that is taken out of production, never to be made again. This is usually followed by a scarcity of the piece and an increase in value on the secondary market.

Secondary Market – the source for buying and selling collectibles according to basic supply-and-demand principles. Popular pieces that are sold out or have been retired can appreciate in value far above the original issue price. Pieces are sold through newspaper ads, collector newsletters, the Internet and swap & sells at collector gatherings.

Variations – pieces that have color, design or printed text changes from the "original" piece, whether intentional or not. Some are minor changes, while some are important enough to affect the piece's value on the secondary market.

Version – denotes the particular carving of a piece. Usually, Version 1 has an issue size of 5,000 and may be more experimental in design than the later version (Version Infinity).

Index – Numerical

Index – Numerical

Index – Alphabetical

All Harmony Kingdom pieces are listed below in alphabetical order. The first number refers to the piece's location within the Value Guide section and the second to the box in which it is pictured on that page.

ACKNOWLEDGEMENTS

CheckerBee Publishing would like to extend a special thanks to Todd Garen, Jane Kropp and the many collectors and retailers who contributed their valuable time to assist us with this book. Also many thanks to the great people at The Harmony Ball Company.

This form is not for use if membership kit is purchased directly through retailer.

Name (please print) _____

Address _____

City _____

State/Province/County_____

ZIP/Postal Code _____

Country _____

Daytime Phone _____

E-Mail_____

Membership # (if previous member) _____

Your HK Retailer_____

To discover the hidden secrets of Harmony Kingdom, become a member of The Royal Watch Collector's Club by mailing your club application (see reverse) to the appropriate address below:

North & South America (except Canada)
Harmony Ball Company, Attn: Royal Watch
232 Neilston Street, Columbus, Ohio 43215
United States
RoyalWatch@HarmonyBall.com
Phone 614-469-0600

Canada
Amyot & Watt Ltd., Attn: Royal Watch
?00 Ridgeway Drive, Unit 17, Mississauga, Ontario L5L 5Y6
Canada
Amyot_Watt@compuserve.com
Phone 800-240-4175

Worldwide (except The Americas)
Harmony International Ltd., Attn: Royal Watch
Wimberley Mills, Knapp Lane, Brimscombe, Stroud, Glos.
GL5 2TH United Kingdom
harmonyho@msn.com
Phone +44 (0) 1453 885722

I am paying $40 [USD] (U.S. Residents), $60 (Residents of The Americas except the U.S. and Canada) annual membership dues by:

☐ Check (payable to Harmony Ball Company)

☐ MasterCard® ☐ VISA® ☐ Discover®

*Ohio residents add 5.75% sales tax • New York residents add 4% sales tax plus applicable local tax

I am paying $60 [CND] (Canadian Residents) annual membership dues by:

☐ Cheque (payable to Amyot & Watt Ltd.)

☐ MasterCard® ☐ VISA®

I am paying £24.95 (U.K. Residents), £29.50 (Residents of Europe except the U.K.), £37.50 (Worldwide Residents except Europe and The Americas) annual membership dues by:

☐ Cheque (payable to Harmony International Ltd.)

☐ MasterCard® ☐ VISA®

Card Number _____

Exp. Date _____Cardholder Name _____

Signature _____

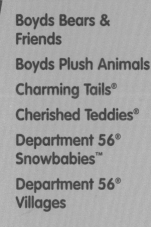

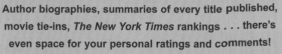
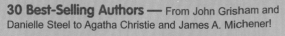